the five points of calvinism

enlarged edition

Edwin H. Palmer

BAKER BOOK HOUSE
Grand Rapids, Michigan

Copyright 1972 by
Baker Book House Company
ISBN: 0-8010-6926-2
Library of Congress
Catalog Card Number: 72-85671

Second printing, January 1982

Enlarged edition issued 1980

.

/

PHOTOLITHOPRINTED BY CUSHING - MALLOY, INC.
ANN ARBOR, MICHIGAN, UNITED STATES OF AMERICA

foreword

The title *The Five Points of Calvinism* can be misleading. For Calvinism does not have five points; and, neither is Calvin the author of the five points.

First of all, Calvinism is not restricted to five points: it has thousands of points. The first word that Calvinism suggests to most people is predestination; and if they have a modicum of theological knowledge, the other four points follow. But this is wrong. Calvinism is much broader than five points. It is not even primarily concerned with the five points. In the first catechism which Calvin drew up (1537), predestination is only briefly mentioned. In the Confession of Faith, drawn up in the same year, there is no mention of it at all. In another catechism and four confessions attributed to Calvin, the doctrine is mentioned only in passing. And in the first edition of his monumental work, *The Institutes*, it is given no important place even when he treats the matter of salvation. It was only in later editions, after attacks had been made on the grace of God, that he enlarged upon predestination.

Calvinism has an unlimited number of points: it is as broad as the Bible. Does the Bible teach about the Trinity? Then, Calvinism does. Does the Bible deal with the deity of Christ, the covenant of grace, justification by faith, sanctification, the second coming of Christ, the inerrancy of Scripture and the world-and-life view? Then, Calvinism does, too. For John Calvin's goal in his preaching, teaching, and writing was to expound all the Word of God — and the Word of God alone. *Scriptura tota: Scriptura sola.* Calvinism is an attempt to express all the Bible and only the Bible. To restrict it to five points is to misjudge and dishonor the man and movement that bears the name Calvin.

Not only can the word *five* be misleading in the name *The Five Points of Calvinism*, but also the word *Calvinism*. At first glance, many believe that Calvin is the author of the five points. Such a misconception ignores the fact that Calvin simply expounded the Bible. Calvin did not invent a new teaching any more than Columbus invented America or Newton the law of gravity. As Columbus and Newton merely discovered what had existed all along, so Calvin uncovered truths that had been in the Bible all the time. And Calvin was not the first nor the last to uncover these Biblical truths. Many others confessed them, too. From Augustine to Gottschalk to Spurgeon; from Lutherans to Baptists to Dominicans; from Dutch to Scottish to French; from individuals to associations to church confessions; from laymen to hymn-writers to theologians. The name Calvinism has often been used, not because Calvin was the first or sole teacher, but because after the long silence of the Middle Ages, he was the most eloquent and systematic expositor of these truths. To the novitiate, however, it seemed as if Calvin originated them.

It is these truths of the sovereign grace of God that are dealt with in this booklet. One easy way to remember them is by the memory-crutch T-U-L-I-P; Total depravity, Unconditional election, Limited atonement, Irresistible grace, and Perseverance of the saints.

contents

1
total depravity

Since there are so many misconceptions concerning total depravity, it is necessary first of all to state what the doctrine is not; and then, second, to state what it is.

I. WHAT IT IS NOT

A. It is not absolute depravity

Sometimes the word *depravity* coupled with the word *total* gives the impression that man is as bad as possible — as evil as he can be, somewhat like the devil.

But total depravity is not the same as absolute depravity. Absolute depravity means that a person expresses his depravity to the nth degree at all times. Not only are all of his thoughts, words, and deeds sinful, but they are as vicious as possible. To be totally depraved, however, does not mean that a person is as intensively evil as possible, but as extensively evil as possible. It is not that he cannot commit a worse crime; rather, it is that nothing that he does is good. Evil pervades every faculty of his soul and every sphere of his life. He is unable to do a single thing that is good.

To illustrate: When boys lie they often tell little lies. Those lies could be a lot worse. Yet what they do is wrong. There is no good in their lying at all. Therefore they are evil. But they are not as bad as they could be.

Or when children hurt each other, they often do it by laughing at another or hitting or shoving; but they could gouge out their eyes with scissors or drive needles under their fingernails.

Some grown-ups call others "blockheads" and "scum"; but they could knock out their teeth instead of calling names.

Hitler was a vicious brute; yet, even he spared some French villages at the plea of a priest.

Kitty Genovese was left to die in New York in the sight of twenty-eight people. This apathy — this reluctance to get involved — is abominable; and yet the twenty-eight could have helped kill her. They did not. They were not as bad as possible. During King Saul's reign a transition came about: "The Spirit of the Lord departed from Saul, and an evil spirit from the Lord tormented him" (I Sam. 16:14). In other words, in the earlier portion of his reign he did not act in as evil a way as in the latter portion.

Even those who are in the process of committing the unpardonable sin (Heb. 6:4-8) did not act at one time as vilely as possible, but "were once enlightened, and tasted of the heavenly gift, and were made partakers of the Holy Spirit."

There have always been hypocrites in the church: those having a form of godliness but denying the power thereof (II Tim. 3:5), and even preaching and performing miracles, as in the case of Judas. These hypocrites could have put away all semblance of charity and directly persecuted people. They did not.

Not only are the sins of man not as bad as they might be, but neither are they as comprehensive as they might be. One man does not commit all possible sins. We all violate God's commandments in thought, but not all of them in action. Everybody has hated, for example; but not everyone has murdered. Almost everyone has lusted, but not all have committed actual adultery. The reason for this moderation of sin is that God, through His common grace (that is, grace that is extended to unbelievers), restrains the evil that people would do. For example, in Genesis 20 we read that King Abimelech did not sin as much as he could have, because God prevented him from committing adultery with Sarah, Abraham's wife. And Paul writes the Thessalonians that "the mystery of lawlessness is at work already" (II Thess. 2:7), but counteracting this evil spirit is "one who is at present restraining it."

B. It is not a complete absence of relative good

Not only is it true that the unregenerate does not commit sins in the worst way possible, nor all sorts of sins, but it is also true that he is capable of doing a certain amount of good — if you rightly understand the word *good*.

The Heidelberg Catechism gives a clear definition of good. In answer to the question: "But what are good works?" the Catechism answers: "Only those which are done from true faith, according to the law of God, and to His glory" (Question and Answer 91). According to the Catechism, then, three elements go to make up *truly* good works: true faith, conformity to the law of God, and a proper motive. A *relatively* good work, on the other hand, may have the correct outward form but not be done from a true faith or to the glory of God. Thus non-Christians can perform relatively good deeds, even though they themselves are totally depraved.

Suppose, for example, that an unbeliever steals $5,000 from a bank and then writes a check for $1,000 to the Red Cross in order to gain praise. His giving may be outwardly in conformity with the law of God; but because it does not spring from faith and because it lacks the motive of glorifying God, it is sinful. It is only a relatively good deed.

Albert Schweitzer is an example of one who denied Biblical Christianity and yet who put to shame many an orthodox Christian by his love and kindness. He sacrificed three promising careers and gave up the culture of Europe in order that he might work and suffer with the blacks in Africa. As a philosopher, New Testament scholar, and widely acclaimed organist, he felt that he was like Dives, clothed in purple and fine linen, living luxuriously day by day, as long as there were Lazaruses in Africa whose sores were still being licked by dogs. By a life of sacrificial ministering to the sick in the heart of Africa, he lived an exemplary life of relative good. His outward actions conformed to the law of love; but because he did not believe in the Triune God and did not have the proper motive of glory for God, his actions could be called truly good only in a relative sense.

For other examples of relative good, consider the non-Christian soldier who exemplifies courage and love in combat by throwing himself on a grenade, thereby saving his buddies.

Or the non-Christian who risks his life by dashing before an oncoming truck to rescue a child.

Or a blaspheming pagan who helps a beggar.

Or the Jew who donates his large estate for public recreation.

Or the Unitarian who gives $100,000 for a science building at a university.

Or the elderly gentleman who lives across the street from you and who will have nothing to do with the church. He is respectable, keeps a neat home, trims the lawn, loves his wife, gives candy to the neighborhood children, and does not swear.

In all of these examples two necessary ingredients of good works are missing: faith in Jesus Christ and the motive of doing them to the glory of the Triune God. Thus they may be called relatively good works rather than truly good works.[1]

The Bible gives examples of relative good. The Old Testament mentions three kings, for example – Jehu, Jehoash, and Amaziah – who did not truly fear God, who were reprobate. Yet of Jehu God says: "Because you did well in doing that which is right in mine eyes . . . your sons of the fourth generation will sit on the throne of Israel" (II Kings 10:30). Of Jehoash the Bible says that he "did that which was right in the eyes of Jehovah" (II Kings 12:2). And the writer repeats the same words for King Amaziah. Thus these kings did things that were pleasing before God, even though they themselves were ultimately lost.

In the New Testament the fact that the reprobate do good is expressly stated by Christ when He commanded the disciples to love not only their friends, but also their enemies. He reasoned: "And if you do good to them that do good to you, what reward do you have? for even sinners do the same" (Luke 6:33). In other words, Christ says that the nonelect do good. Again, this may not be taken to mean that they do that which is truly good, but that they perform a relative good.

And Paul writes to the Romans (2:14) that the "Gentiles who do not have the law do by nature the things of the law." They do not know Jesus Christ, they do not have the law of the Old Testament, and yet they do things which are outwardly in accordance with the law of God – things which are pleasing to God in a relative sense.

Thus we see that total depravity does not mean that each man is the epitome of the devil. For, as a matter of fact, man does not commit all the sins possible; and those he does commit are not always as bad as possible. Furthermore, we see that he can even perform a certain amount of relative good. How grateful

---

[1]The title of Article XIV of the Belgic Confession mentions the "truly good" when it speaks of fallen man's "incapacity to perform what is truly good." The Canons of Dort speak of "saving good" (III–IV, 3). These terms can be misleading. For even the regenerate's deeds are not "truly good," since neither his faith nor motive is completely perfect. No person on earth loves God with all of his heart, mind, and soul. And yet, of course, the actions of the regenerate Christian are of a completely different character from those of the unbeliever. The faith and motive are there even if in an imperfect way. Neither is it accurate to speak of "saving good," since the Christian is not saved by good works, but by Christ.

we can be to God for the exercise of His common grace, by which He not only restrains the evil in the unregenerate, but also enables them to do this relative good!

II. WHAT IT IS

A. Positively: only and always sinning

Although we assert that natural man — one who has not been regenerated by the Holy Spirit — can do relative good, it is necessary to reemphasize that even this relative good is not fundamentally "truly good" in God's sight. The reason for this is, as the Belgic Confession puts it, that the motive of love and faith is missing. In fact, that relative good is basically, in the deepest sense, nothing else than sin and evil.

Total depravity means that natural man is never able to do any good that is fundamentally pleasing to God, and, in fact, does evil all the time. This is the clear witness of Scripture.

In Genesis 6:5 we are told "that the wickedness of man was great on the earth, and that every imagination of the thoughts of his heart was only evil continually." Note carefully the description of the wickedness. It was great. It penetrated to the deepest recesses of man. Not only to his heart, not only to the thoughts of his heart, but also to the imagination of the thoughts of his heart. Such innermost attitudes, according to the Bible, were only evil and that was continually so — all the time. Genesis 8:21 adds the information that this was so not only when man was fully matured but also from his youth.

Jeremiah says that "the heart is deceitful above all things and desperately wicked. Who can know it?" (17:9). The testimony of most Christians jibes with Jeremiah's. Even after a person has become a Christian, and therefore knows better, it is dismaying how hypocritical, deceitful, and desperately wicked his heart is.

The Psalmist says that this depravity applies even to babies: "Behold, I was shapen in iniquity, and in sin did my mother conceive me" (51:5). This does not mean that sexual intercourse is evil, but rather that from conception and birth man is polluted with sin because of the fall of Adam.

In unequivocal tones Paul, quoting from Psalms 14 and 53, says, "There is none righteous, no, not one. There is none who understands; there is none who seeks after God. They have all gone astray; together they have become worthless. There is no one who does good, no, not even one. . . . There is no fear of God before their eyes" (Rom. 3:10-18).

Thus depravity is extensive rather than intensive. Man does not sin in as many ways as possible, nor in the worst way possible, and can even perform a certain amount of relative good, but he does sin in everything that he does. He does not do a single work that is thoroughly pleasing to God.

B. Negatively: total inability

Another way of describing total depravity is to call it *total inability*. As a matter of fact, many prefer this term to *total depravity*, since the latter term leads some to think that man is as bad as he can be. The term *total inability*, however, suffers from being too negative. It suggests that the sinfulness of man is a lack rather than a positive characteristic. But the term is very useful in driving home the fact of the inability of man to do, understand, or even desire the good. Let us now look at this threefold inability of man.

1. *Man cannot do the good*

The Belgic Confession is very Scriptural when it declares natural man's "incapacity to perform what is truly good." The Canons of Dort are likewise Scriptural when they confess that "all men are . . . incapable of saving good."

In speaking of the total moral inability of the unregenerate to do good, Jesus once asked: "Can we pick grapes from thornbushes or figs from thistles?" His answer was: "No, every good tree bears good fruit, and the bad tree bears bad fruit. A good tree cannot bear bad fruit, nor can a bad tree bear good fruit" (Matt. 7:17-18). In other words, the unregenerate cannot do what is truly good.

Writing in a similar vein Paul once said: "No one speaking by the Holy Spirit ever says, 'Jesus be damned'; and no one is able to say, 'Jesus is Lord' except by the Holy Spirit" (I Cor. 12: 3).

On another occasion Jesus gave the secret of the Christian life: the indwelling of Christ (John 15). He used the illustration of a grapevine and its branches. In speaking of the inability to do good works, He said: "Just as the branch is not able by itself to bear fruit — unless it abides in the vine — so neither can you

unless you abide in me. . . . Apart from me you can do nothing"
(John 15:4-5). That's total inability.

In similarly sweeping statements, Paul denies the ability of
the non-Christian to do good when he writes: "The mind of the
flesh [i.e., the unregenerate] is hostile to God, for it is not subject to the law of God; nor can it be; and those who are in the
flesh [i.e., unregenerate] cannot please God" (Rom. 8:7-8).
Read again that threefold description of total depravity or total
inability: the non-Christian is hostile to God, he is not obedient
to the law of God, and it is impossible for him to do good and
please God.

2. Man cannot understand the good

Not only is man unable to do the good by himself, he is not even
able to understand the good. He is as blind as Cyclops with his
one eye burned out. Lydia, for example, heard Paul preach
Christ at the riverside in Philippi. Only after the Lord opened
her heart was she able to give heed to what was said by Paul
(Acts 16:14). Until then, her understanding was darkened, to
use Paul's description of the Ephesian Gentiles (Eph. 4:18).
Or, to use another Pauline illustration, a veil over her heart prevented her from seeing the truth (II Cor. 3:12-18). But when
God operated on her spiritual heart, she could respond to Paul's
preaching.

During the ministry of Jesus, the Jews rejected Him. "He came
to his own and his own did not receive him" (John 1:11). The
trouble was not in the presentation of the truth. The Truth was
there. Jesus was the Son of God incarnate. The Light shone in
the darkness, but the darkness could not comprehend it.

The Son performed miracles and preached to the Jews, but
they blasphemed Him. "Why don't you understand what I say?"
Jesus once asked. He supplied the answer also: "Because you
are not able to hear my word" (John 8:43). Surely, the Jews
heard Jesus with their physical ears. But Jesus was speaking
about their spiritual ears. As He said elsewhere, "By hearing
you will hear but never understand; and seeing you will see but
never perceive" (Matt. 13:14). This explains why some theologians and Bible students can spend most of their lives studying
the Bible and yet reject Jesus Christ as their God, Lord, and
Savior. The cause of rejection is not in the clear testimony of
God's Word. Rather, it is in the blindness, darkness, and hard-

ness of their hearts. If a man is not regenerated, he cannot understand.

One of the clearest passages teaching the inability of natural man to understand the things of God is I Corinthians 1 and 2. Paul says that the word of the cross (i.e., the central message of Christianity) is foolishness to those who go to hell (I Cor. 1:18). By their own "wisdom" they did not come to know God (v. 21). If they could know God by their natural wisdom, then many wise people would be Christians. But such is not the case. The reason that the brilliant minds do not accept Christianity is that all minds are blind, unless they are regenerated. For, as Paul asserts, "the natural man does not receive the things of the Spirit of God for they are foolishness to him; and neither can he understand them, because they are spiritually discerned" (2:14). In other words, without the Holy Spirit one is not able to understand the things of God.

3. *Man cannot desire the good*

Not only is the non-Christian unable to do anything that is truly good, not only is he unable to understand the good, but, worse still, he is not even able to desire the good. It is one thing to have a good goal and not be able to reach it. This inability to reach a good goal is part of the depravity of man. It is another thing to have a good goal, but not even be able to understand what that goal is. This lack of understanding is also a part of man's depravity. But the pit of total depravity is that natural man does not even desire a good goal. He could not care less. That last statement is wrong. He does care: he hates the good and its source, namely, God. This lack of desire for God is both the pit and epitome of man's natural total depravity.

This inability to desire the good, and especially Jesus Christ, is expressed forcefully by Jesus in another of His *cannot* statements (cf. Matt. 7:18; John 3:3; 8:43; and 15:4-5). He said: "No one can come to me unless the Father who sent me draw him" (John 6:44). Shortly after that He repeated the same thought in different words: "No one can come to me unless it has been granted to him by the Father" (John 6:65). Here is *total* depravity: man cannot choose Jesus. He cannot even take the first step to go to Jesus, unless the Father draws him. And this depravity is universal. "No one" can come, says Jesus. Not just some cannot, but none can come. That is universal, total inability.

The most potent evidence that man cannot even desire the good is found in every Biblical illustration of the effect of the initial work of the Holy Spirit: a heart of flesh, birth, creation, and resurrection. These expressions demonstrate with childlike clarity man's total moral inability.

For example, in the Old Testament the unregenerate is described as having a heart that is made of stone (Ezek. 11:19). A stone heart has no life. It is dead; it can do nothing. That is total inability. But God says that He will regenerate His people. He will put a new spirit in them, and then they will have a heart of flesh, that is alive. Then they will have the ability to follow God.

Jesus used the analogy of birth: "Unless one is born again, he cannot see the kingdom of God" (John 3:3). A baby never desires or decides to be born. He never contributes an iota toward his own birth. In the whole process from conception through birth, he is completely passive and totally unable to control his birth. In a similar fashion, the unbeliever cannot take one step toward his rebirth. He must be generated by the Spirit. The Arminian teaches the unnatural concept that a spiritual nonbeing can desire to be born — can believe on Christ and then be born again. But a nonbeing does not exist and therefore can have no desires to go to Christ.

Paul used the illustration of creation. He said that if anyone is in Christ he is a new creation (II Cor. 5:17; Gal. 6:15). Nonbeing — nothingness — can never produce itself. The very concept of creation necessarily implies total passivity and inability on the part of the object that is to be created. What is true in the physical realm is also true in the spiritual realm: individuals are totally unable to make of themselves new creations in Christ.

Paul also used the analogy of the resurrection when in Ephesians 2:1 he wrote, "And he made you alive when you were dead through your trespasses and sins." In the fifth verse he says: "Even when we were dead through our trespasses God made us alive together with Christ" (cf. Col. 2:13). Some very fine Christians interpet these verses as meaning that man is injured or sick but not dead, for they say that man still has the ability to ask God's help for salvation. Man has the power to believe or not to believe. He is not really dead; for if he were, he could not ask for help. He is only sick. Yes, full of sin, sick with sin, but he can still ask the doctor for help. But the Calvinist holds to the plain teaching of Scripture and says: "No; he is dead.

He cannot even open his mouth. Nor does he have any desire to call a doctor to help him. He is dead."

The Arminian compares the unregenerate to one who jumps out of a second story window, cracks three ribs, breaks his leg, and still lives. The man knows that he is seriously injured and therefore needs a doctor. In fact, he can call for help from a passer-by or drag himself to the phone to call the doctor. He wants to be made whole and well.

The Calvinist, however, would compare man to one who jumps off the top of the Empire State Building and is spattered over the sidewalk. Even if there were anything left of him when he landed, he could not know that he needed help, let alone cry out for it. That man is dead — lifeless — and cannot even desire to be made whole.

Or, to use another example: the theory that gives man a little credit for his salvation by granting him the ability to believe, pictures man as drowning. His head is bobbing up and down in the water as he flails his arms, trying to keep above water. If someone doesn't save him, he will die. He may have his lungs partially filled with water, even lose consciousness for a moment or two, but he still has enough presence of mind and ability to wave and yell to the lifeguard to save him. If he calls to the guard, the guard will rescue him.

The Biblical picture, however, is of a man at the bottom of the ocean in the Marianas trench, more than thirty-five thousand feet deep. The weight of the water on top of him is six tons for every square inch. He has been there for a thousand years and the sharks have eaten his heart. In other words, the man is dead and is totally unable to ask any lifeguard to save him. If he is to be saved, then a miracle must occur. He must be brought back to life and to the surface, and then he can ask the guard to rescue him.

And that is the picture of the sinner. He is dead in his sins and trespasses (Eph. 2:1, 5). He does not want to be made whole, let alone even know that he should be made whole. He is dead.

When Christ called to Lazarus to come out of the grave, Lazarus had no life in him so that he could hear, sit up, and emerge. There was not a flicker of life in him. If he was to be able to hear Jesus calling him and to go to Him, then Jesus would have to make him alive. Jesus did resurrect him and then Lazarus could respond.

These illustrations reveal the most central issue between the Arminian and the Calvinist, what Martin Luther even said was the hinge on which the whole Reformation turned.[2] The Arminian — and we write kindly of him even though we find him unbiblical at this point — believes that Christ died for sin and that no man can make even the smallest contribution to the payment for his sins. So far, so good. "Jesus paid it all, all to Him I owe."

But the real nub of the matter is that the Arminian then goes on to say that the unsaved is able in his own strength, with an assist of the Holy Spirit, to ask Jesus to save him. And once he has asked, then he will be born again.

The Biblical Calvinist, however, says no. The Arminian has the cart before the horse. Man is dead in sins and trespasses, not just sick or injured but nevertheless alive. No, the unsaved, the unregenerate, is spiritually dead (Eph. 2). He is unable to ask for help unless God changes his heart of stone into a heart of flesh, and makes him alive spiritually (Eph. 2:5). Then, once he is born again, he can for the first time turn to Jesus, expressing sorrow for his sins and asking Jesus to save him.

The question is: Is God the author of redemption alone or also of faith? Does God contribute the substitutionary sacrifice of Christ, and man contribute his faith? Or is faith also a gift of God (Eph 2:8)? Does salvation depend partly on God (the giving of Christ on the cross) or wholly on God (the giving of Christ to die for us plus the giving of our faith)?

Does man keep just a little bit of glory for himself — the ability to believe? Or does all the glory go to God? The teaching of total depravity is that God gets all the glory, and man none.

Conclusion

There are three lessons to be drawn from the Biblical teaching of the total depravity of man.

---

[2]*The Bondage of the Will*, trans. J. I. Packer and O. R. Johnston, p. 319. The title of this book is another good description of total depravity or total inability. The will is not free: it is in bondage or slavery to the devil. It is "like a beast standing between two riders. If God rides, it wills and goes where God wills. . . . If Satan rides, it wills and goes where Satan wills. Nor may it choose to which rider it will run, or which it will seek; but the riders themselves fight to decide who shall have and hold it" (pp. 103-104). This excellent book of Luther against Erasmus' unbiblical ideas shows what a good "Calvinist" Luther was.

1. *Total depravity explains the troubles in our world*

It is the innate hatred against God and man that is the root of student violence, the burning, rioting, and looting in racial disturbances, anarchy, self-centered strikes, dope-peddling, crime, and the general chaos that Americans and the world are heading for.

Without being simplistic or naive, it can be stated that society will not solve these problems fundamentally until people are born again and turn to Jesus Christ. For the Bible tells us that man is not spiritually alive; and the result is that "there is no one who does good, no, not even one; their throat is an open grave; their tongues are full of deceit; snake poison is on their lips; their mouths are full of cursing and bitterness, their feet run fast to shed blood; wherever they go there is destruction and misery; they don't know the way of peace; they have no fear of God" (Rom. 3:12-18).

And it is going to get worse before it gets better, so prophesies the Bible. In the latter days, Satan will be loosed for a while, and it will seem as though all hell has broken loose.

This does not mean that the conversion of the whole world would solve all the problems. For born-again Christians are still sinful, even though they have been basically changed. The world needs more than conversion: it needs Christians who put Christian principles to work in politics, labor, economics, and society in general.

But this teaching of total depravity should warn the Christian not to be surprised at the hateful, destructive, rebellious, anarchistic mentality of the present world; and it should point us to the need of the gospel in solving these problems.

2. *A knowledge of total depravity should also teach us that we are thoroughly bad and in a terrible state of affairs unless God helps us*

When anyone learns from the Bible about the enormity of his sin, he should want to run to God and plead, "Help me, Jesus. I'm bad and sinful. I've done wrong. I'm no good. Save me, Jesus."

When he does that, then a third truth will follow.

3. *A knowledge of total depravity will teach a person that if he has a desire to ask God to help him, it is only because it is*

*God who is working within him to will and to do according
to His good pleasure (Phil. 2:12, 13)*

He will know that not only did Jesus die for his sins, but that
God even put it in his heart to believe on Jesus. Then he will
cry, "How good can God be?" He not only sends Christ to bear
hellish punishment for me, but He even makes me, who really
did not love Jesus, want to love Him and believe in Him. What
a good God!

> " 'Tis not that I did choose Thee,
> For, Lord, that could not be;
> This heart would still refuse Thee,
> Hadst Thou not chosen me."

"Thank you, Lord, for saving my soul."

Helps for Leaders on the Use of the Discussion Questions

1. Everybody has different interests and backgrounds; hence all
   the questions will not speak to everyone. So be selective and
   choose the ones that you can get excited about. There are
   more than enough for one session.
2. When someone answers the question correctly, perhaps right
   at the start, do not say: "Fine; now we will go to the next
   question." Rather, play the devil's advocate: ask the others if
   they agree with that, and ask why they agree. The most
   instructive learning will come when there is disagreement
   about the answers. Let the others fight it out. Do not, as a
   leader, step in and solve the problem right away. But at the
   end be sure to give what you think is the truth. Do not leave
   them hanging, but do let them argue with each other for
   a while.
3. Never laugh at or ridicule any answer, however foolish you
   may think it is. To do so is the surest way of stopping all
   further discussion. People will then be afraid that you are
   going to ridicule them if they should make a mistake. Without agreeing with the error suggested, it is usually possible
   to find some truth in the answer given. It is better to pick
   that up and then gently show where the person was wrong.
4. Do not ask questions that demand a yes or no for an answer.
   Then you have a dud. Silence. If you do ask that kind of
   question, follow it with "Why?" Even though you know all the

answers, play dumb and have them explain why they think as they do.

DISCUSSION QUESTIONS

1. Can Paul be considered a Calvinist even though he lived hundreds of years before Calvin?
2. What is Calvinism? Are you sure? Check your answer with the foreword.
3. Is it wise to call Scriptural teachings after a man, such as Calvinism, Lutheranism or Wesleyanism? Is there any harm in it?
4. What word will help you recall all the five points of Calvinism?
5. Name the five points.
6. Which two articles in the Belgic Confession of Faith deal with total depravity? (See pp. 98-100.) Is there any idea here that is fresh for you? What is it?
7. Read Questions 6-9 in the Heidelberg Catechism. Discuss them thoroughly.
8. Read the Canons of Dort (III–IV, 1-4) and the Rejection of Errors (4-5). (See the back of the *Psalter Hymnal* of the Christian Reformed Church.)
9. Read the outstanding statement of total depravity in the Westminster Confession of Faith (VI and IX). (See pp. 101-108.)
10. What is total depravity? Describe it negatively and positively.
11. Why is it called *total?*
12. What is the difference between total depravity and absolute depravity?
13. What is common grace? Mention at least three aspects of it. Read what the Christian Reformed Church said about it in the 1924 *Acts of Synod.*
14. Is the Christian totally depraved?
15. You may be acquainted with Golding's novel *The Lord of the Flies.* What does it have to say about man's depravity?
16. Give some examples of total depravity in recent news or among your friends.
17. What is meant by "relative good"?
18. Why is the so-called relative good not fundamentally and basically pleasing to God, but really and basically evil?
19. Take the life of some noble, well-known non-Christian. Is he all bad? When you answer, be sure you define what you mean by good and bad.
20. Give examples of people doing the right thing outwardly but from a wrong motive. Are they doing good or evil? Why?
21. Can the unregenerate love God?
22. Turn to your Bible and tell what the following texts say about total depravity:
    a. Psalm 51:5
    b. John 6:44, 65
    c. John 8:34
    d. Romans 8:7, 8
    e. I Corinthians 2:14

23. Would you compare the unregenerate to a sick man or to a dead man? Why?
24. Do people in hell want to get out and be where Jesus is in heaven? Explain.
25. Do people in hell increase their guilt?
26. What does the Biblical teaching of total depravity say about the idea of a better world through more education? or a higher standard of living? or psychology?
27. Evaluate this statement: Man is like a geode: rough on the outside, but exquisite on the inside.
28. If you are not a Christian and are totally depraved, how can you ever believe in Christ?
29. Should ministers preach on such a pessimistic subject as total depravity? Why?

2
unconditional election

When the terms *predestination* or *divine election* are used, a shiver goes down many people's spines; and they picture man caught in the clutches of a horrible, impersonal Fate. Others — even those who believe in the doctrine — think it is something that is all right for the theological classroom, but that it has no place at all in the pulpit. They would rather have people study it in secret in the privacy of the home.[1]

Such an attitude is unbiblical and is based on a lack of knowledge of what the Bible says about election. For election, instead of being a horrible doctrine, when understood Biblically, is perhaps the finest, warmest, most joyous teaching in all the Bible. It will cause the Christian to praise and thank God for His goodness in saving him, a good for nothing, hell-deserving sinner.

In order to understand what the Bible says about divine election, let us look at:

      I. What it is.
     II. Its Biblical basis.
    III. Some clarifications.
    IV. Practical advantages.

I. WHAT IT IS

In order to see clearly what unconditional election is, it will be helpful to understand the meaning of some terms:

A. Foreordination

Foreordination means God's sovereign plan, whereby He decides

---

[1]Since predestination is associated so intimately with John Calvin, it is most instructive to see the humble, pious, God-fearing attitude he had toward the subject. It is so delightfully Biblical and down to earth, I have quoted him at length in the back of the book. See pp. 95-97.

all that is to happen in the entire universe. Nothing in this world happens by chance. God is in back of everything. He decides and causes all things to happen that do happen. He is not sitting on the sidelines wondering and perhaps fearing what is going to happen next. No, He has foreordained everything "after the counsel of his will" (Eph. 1:11): the moving of a finger, the beating of a heart, the laughter of a girl, the mistake of a typist — even sin. (See Gen. 45:5-8; Acts 4:27-28; and chap. 6 of this book.)

B. Predestination

Predestination is a part of foreordination. While foreordination refers to God's plans for everything that ever happens, predestination is that part of foreordination that refers to man's eternal destiny: heaven or hell. Predestination is composed of two parts: election and reprobation. Election concerns those who go to heaven, and reprobation concerns those who go to hell.

C. Unconditional election

To understand this term, consider each word:

1. Election

We all know what a national election is: a choosing among candidates of one to be the president of the United States. To elect means to choose, to select, to opt. Divine election means that God chooses some to go to heaven. Others are passed by and they will go to hell.

2. Unconditional

A conditional election is an election that is conditioned on something in the person being elected. For example, all political elections are conditional elections. The voter's choice is conditioned by something that the candidate is or has promised. Some candidates promise the sky if they are elected. Others promise only to be a good elected representative and to do what is right. Still others appeal to the fact that they are Negroes, Italians, Jews, or Anglo-Saxons. Thus human elections are always conditional elections, the choice of the voter being based on the promises and character of the one to be elected.

But, amazing as it may seem, divine election is always an unconditional election. God never bases His choice on what man thinks, says, does, or is. We do not know what God bases His choice on, but it is not on anything that is in man. He does not see something good in a particular man, something that he does that makes God decide to choose him.

And isn't that wonderful? Suppose that God's election to heaven was based on something that we had to be or think or do. Who then would ever be saved? What man can stand before God and say that he has ever done one thing for a single moment that was really good in the deepest sense of that term? We are all dead in our sins and trespasses (Eph. 2). There is none that does good, no, not one (Rom. 3). If God's election were based on a single good thing that is to be found in us, then no one would be elected. Then none would go to heaven; all would go to hell. For no one is good. So, thank God for His unconditional election.

To make absolutely clear what is meant by unconditional election, it is necessary to refer to Arminianism. I do not like to do that, for it may seem that I am hostile to Arminians. On the contrary, I believe that Arminians may be born-again Christians.[2] They believe that there is a Triune God, that Jesus is God, and that He died for the sins of man. They hold to salvation by faith alone and not by good works. Therefore, all true believers — those who trust in Jesus as their Savior — should find real Christian fellowship with Arminians. They are one in Christ.

Although Arminians are sincere Christians, they are completely wrong in the matter of **T-U-L-I-P**: Total depravity, Unconditional election, Limited atonement, Irresistible grace, and Perseverance of the saints. And the only reason I mention Arminianism is to show the Biblical teachings more clearly. For white is never so white as against black. And so the Biblical truths of Calvinism are never so clear as against the erroneous ideas of the Arminian. Thus, it is with reluctance that we mention Arminianism so much, but we do it out of love and appreciation for them. We simply desire to present the full joy of the Christian faith and not to have it clouded by the erroneous idea of conditional election.

---

[2]Arminianism was named after a Dutch theologian, Jacobus Arminius, who lived from 1560 to 1609. He developed the Five Points of Arminianism, against which the international church council of Dort (Holland) spoke out in 1618-19.

According to the Arminian, divine election — and they believe in election — is a conditional one. They think that God foresees who will believe on Christ, and then on the basis of that fore-knowledge God decides to elect the believers to heaven. They believe that at times the natural, nonregenerate man has enough goodness in him so that if the Holy Spirit assists him he will want to choose Jesus. Man chooses God, and then God chooses man. God's choice is conditioned upon man's choice. Thus the Arminian teaches conditional election; whereas the Calvinist teaches unconditional election.

II. ITS BIBLICAL BASIS

The Five Points of Calvinism all tie together. He who accepts one of the points will accept the other points. Unconditional election necessarily follows from total depravity.

If men are totally depraved and if some are still saved, then it is obvious that the reason some are saved and some are lost rests entirely with God. All of mankind would remain lost if left to itself and not chosen by God to be saved. For by nature man is dead spiritually (Eph. 2) and not just sick. He has no spiritual life or goodness in him. He cannot do anything that is truly good — no, not so much as even understand the things of God and Christ, let alone desire Christ or salvation. Only when the Holy Spirit regenerates man and makes him alive spiritually can man have faith in Christ and be saved. Therefore, if total depravity is Biblically true, then faith and consequent salvation come only when the Holy Spirit goes to work through regeneration. And the decision as to which persons He will work in must rest entirely, one hundred percent, with God, since man, being spiritually dead, cannot ask for help. This, then, is unconditional election: God's choice does not rest on anything that man does.

A. John 6:37, 39

Jesus promised His listeners, "All that the Father gives me will come to me, and whoever comes to me I will never drive away. . . . And this is the will of him who sent me, that I shall lose none of all that he has given me, but raise them up at the last day."

It is clearly seen that those who will be raised up at the last day — all true believers — are given to Christ by the Father. And only those whom the Father gives to Christ can come to Him. Salvation is entirely in the hands of the Father. He it is who gives them to Jesus to be saved. Once they have been given to Jesus, then Jesus will see to it that none of them will be lost. Thus salvation depends entirely upon the Father's giving some to Christ. This is nothing else than unconditional election.

B. John 15:16

Christ said, "You did not choose me, but I chose you."

If ever a text was clear in pointing out unconditional election, this is the one. The Arminian says that he chooses Christ. Christ says, "No, you did not choose me. Rather, I chose you."

Now it is true that the Christian chooses Christ. He believes on Him. It was his decision. And yet Christ says, "No, you did not choose me." Christ's negative remark is just a forceful way of saying that although a Christian may think that he is the decisive factor in choosing Christ, the truth is that ultimately it is Christ who chose the believer. And then, after that, the believer chose Christ. We think that we do all the good things in life, such as believe on Christ; but we must remember that it is God who is working in us both to will and to do according to His good pleasure (Phil. 2:12, 13).

There is a hymn that expresses this beautifully:

> I sought the Lord, and afterward I knew
> He moved my soul to seek Him, seeking me;
> It was not that I found, O Saviour true;
> No, I was found of thee. . . .
> 'Twas not so much that I on Thee took hold,
> As Thou, dear Lord, on me.
> I find, I walk, I love; but O the whole
> Of love is but my answer, Lord, to Thee!
> For Thou wert long beforehand with my soul;
> Always, Thou lovedst me.

That hymn is completely Biblical. It expresses precisely what Christ said to His followers, "You did not choose me, but I chose you." It is what John wrote in his first letter, "We love, because he first loved us." God's love is prior to man's. This is God's sovereign electing love.

> 'Tis not that I did choose Thee,
> For, Lord, that could not be;
> This heart would still refuse Thee,
> Hadst Thou not chosen me.

C. Acts 13:48

Luke reported, "As many as were ordained to eternal life believed."

Here is another text with stunning clarity for whoever will read the Bible without preconceived notions about election. Luke writes of the conversions in Antioch where Paul and Barnabas had been preaching. In telling about the results of their ministry, he uses the words of the above text.

This has bothered Arminians so much that their theologians have tried to twist the words around to read, "As many as believed were ordained to eternal life"; and the forerunner of Unitarianism, Socinus (1539-1604), actually did translate them in that way! But this does complete violence to the text. Such a translation would nicely fit the Arminian theory of God foreseeing who would believe and then ordaining them. But the Bible says the direct opposite: "As many as were ordained to eternal life believed." The stark simplicity of this text is astounding.

D. II Thessalonians 2:13

The apostle Paul stated, "But we have to always thank God for you, brothers, loved by the Lord, because in the beginning God chose you for salvation through sanctification by the Spirit and faith in the truth."

Note first of all that the Thessalonians are said to have been loved by the Lord. This is electing love already. This term "loved by" is never used of the unbeliever, the world, in any passage of the Bible. God never calls Judas or the rejecting world the "ones loved by the Lord." That is a term reserved for those who love Jesus and who are saved by His death. Already this is an indication of the eternal, selecting love of God.

Then note that Paul expressly says that God chose the Thessalonians, implying that He passed over others.

Further, Paul writes that God chose them from the beginning; that is, from before the foundation of the world (Eph. 1:4) — from eternity.

Someone may say, "To be sure, He chose them from eternity, He foreordained who would go to heaven; but He did it on the basis of foreknowledge. God foresaw who would believe on Christ and on that basis He chose them."

But such reasoning ignores the plain teaching of Paul. Paul

does not say that God chose the Thessalonians because they were made holy or because they believed. On the contrary, he says the exact opposite. God chose them "for salvation." Some of the modern versions translate it, "God chose you to find salvation" (New English Bible); or "God chose you from the beginning to be saved" (Jerusalem Bible). Salvation comes only by faith; so when Paul says that God chose the Thessalonians "to be saved," this, of course, implies that God chose to give them the only means for getting that salvation, namely, faith. If God chose to give someone the end result without giving him the means to obtain it, the choice is meaningless.

Just in case there are still some doubters as to whether or not even faith is a gift of God and not of man's efforts (Eph. 2:8), Paul expressly says that God chose them to be saved "by the sanctifying Spirit and by faith in the truth." In other words, salvation, sanctification, and faith are all one package that comes to the Thessalonians from God.

Thus II Thessalonians teaches a choice by God that is not conditioned by anything in man, either his sanctification or his faith. No, God's election is unconditional.

E. Ephesians 1:4-5

Paul says that God the Father has blessed us with every spiritual blessing, "just as he chose us in him before the foundation of the world, that we should be holy and blameless before him. In love he foreordained us to adoption as sons through Jesus Christ to himself, according to the good pleasure of his will."

Notice how strongly Paul speaks of election. He says that God "chose us," not that we chose God. Then he adds that God "foreordained us." Moreover, the sovereign choice is emphasized by the statement that God chose us "in Christ"; that is, He chose us not because of ourselves but because of Christ Jesus.

Perhaps some Arminian will again attempt to reason that God did foreordain some but that it was based on God's foreknowledge of who would believe. Therefore, the decision rests really with man and not with God. But notice that Paul does not say that God chose us *because* we are holy, but, *in order that* we should be holy and blameless. And holiness includes faith, because there is no holiness without faith. Ephesians 1 is just the opposite of what the Arminian says, and it excludes an election that is based on anything found in us — deeds or faith.

This conclusion is further strengthened when Paul adds that this choice and foreordination were "according to the good pleasure of his will." God did not choose man because He foresaw anything worthwhile in man, such as faith, for then He would have said that He predestined us "according to the foreseen faith of man." Rather, Paul omits any reference to man and says that the reason is to be found in God's "good pleasure" alone. To bring out more forcibly this sovereign choice of God, which was not based on anything in man at all, Paul adds the phrase "of his will." This was not necessary for his reasoning. He said that the choice was according to God's good pleasure. That was sufficient to indicate that God's choice was for reasons entirely within Himself. But then he adds "of his will," which indicates still more strongly the freedom of God's choice, the fact that the reason is to be found in His will alone.

F. Romans 8:29, 30

Paul declares, "For whom God foreknew, he also foreordained to be conformed to the image of his Son . . . and whom he foreordained, these he also called; and whom he called, these he also justified; and whom he justified, these he also glorified."

If ever a verse would seem to support the Arminian concept of foreordination based on foreknowledge, this is it. But it is only a superficial reading that would give any comfort to such an erroneous idea. For the word translated by the older versions as "foreknew" is a Hebrew and Greek idiom meaning "love beforehand." When the Bible says that Adam "knew" Eve, it does not mean for a moment that Adam knew how tall she was and what kind of a temperament she had. No, it means that Adam loved Eve.

And when David says that God "knows the way of the righteous, but that the way of the wicked will perish" (Ps. 1), he is not saying that God knows the righteous and does not know the wicked. God knows everything and everyone, including the wicked. David obviously means that God loves the way of the righteous and hates the way of the wicked, whom He will punish.

Similarly, when God says through Amos, "You only have I known of all the families of the earth" (3:2), He is not denying His omniscience, and saying that He does not know anybody else intellectually. No, this is a figure of speech for saying, "You only have I loved of all the families of the earth."

In the same manner, when Paul says in Romans 8:29, "whom God foreknew, he also foreordained," Paul is using the Biblical idiom of "know" for "love," and he means, "whom God loved beforehand, he foreordained." If "foreknew" here means only an intellectual knowledge, then God does not know everything; for then He would not know those whom He had not foreordained to justification and glorification.

What Paul is saying in Romans 8 is that there is a golden chain of salvation that begins with the eternal, electing love of God and goes on in unbreakable links through foreordination, effectual calling, justification, to final glorification in heaven. Instead of supporting the Arminian view that foreordination is based on foreknowledge, Romans 8 agrees in a most powerful way with the rest of Scripture that foreordination of the believer is based on God's eternal love. Thank God that there is that unbroken chain of salvation. Anyone who believes on Christ can know that he is in it.

G. Romans 9:6-26

All of the previously mentioned texts are excellent ones in showing that God does not elect people because of something in them that attracts God. But the finest statement of all is in Romans 9.

The chief problem of Romans 9–11 is this: How can the Israelites, who had all the blessings of God in the past, be spiritually lost? Has God forgotten His promises to Israel? Paul answers with a firm no. "The word of God has not failed" (9:6). Then he goes on in the rest of the chapter to show that salvation does not come because one is a physical descendant of Abraham, but that it is given by the sovereign grace of God. And that is what we want to show.

The first indication is found in the fact that in 9:7 Paul speaks of the sovereign choice of Isaac over against Ishmael. God spoke out sovereignly and selectively, "In Isaac shall thy seed be called."

Then Paul points to the same sovereign choice in the case of Jacob and Esau. Jacob and Esau had the same parents and were even born at the same time: they were twins. Yet God sovereignly chose Jacob and passed Esau by.

To show that God's choice was not based on foreknowledge, Paul writes that God made His choice known to Rebecca before her twins were born and before they had done anything good or bad (9:11). This was done, says Paul, to show "that the purpose of God according to election might stand, not because of works, but because of him who calls" (9:11). God did not choose Jacob because He foresaw that he would be good or would believe. The source of the choice is not found in man, but in "him who calls," that is, God. To clinch the sovereignty of this choice, God simply states, "Jacob I loved, but Esau I hated" (9:13).

As humans we feel like asking, "But why, God?" and God simply answers with a reiteration of the fact, "Jacob I loved, but Esau I hated," and gives no reason that satisfies a searching human mind.

Paul feels the sense of dissatisfaction that will undoubtedly rise in the minds of those who will hear his letter. He senses that some will very naturally think, "What kind of God is that? He isn't fair — loving one and hating the other even before they were born and before they had a chance to prove themselves." So in the next verse (14) Paul asks the question: "Is God unjust?" That's the nub of it: unconditional election seems to imply an unjust God and therefore it cannot be. So man reasons.

Before we go on to see Paul's answer to this charge, reflect for a moment that this very question Paul asks presupposes unconditional election. The question of injustice in God never, never arises in the Arminian theory. For according to the Arminian, God is not arbitrary in His election, since He foresees who will be good or bad, or who will have faith. God's choice is based on something that man does or believes. His foreordination is entirely fair; it is decided upon the merits of man.

The charge of injustice in God can arise only on the basis of unconditional election; for to man it seems foolish to speak of a good, fair God who simply chooses Jacob and passes Esau by, especially when Jacob is no better or deserving than Esau. It's foolishness, he thinks. God must be unjust. Therefore, the very fact that Paul raises the question of unfairness presupposes that he is speaking about unconditional election. On the Arminian theory of conditional election, there is no possibility of raising the question of injustice. But Paul does, showing that he is teaching unconditional election.

The answer of the infallible Word of God to Paul's question is not to retract the sovereignty of God's election, or to try to give a rational explanation to doubting men. Paul simply states, "God forbid!" Do not ever say or think that God is unjust. He certainly is not. He is a good, holy God, and not unjust for a moment.

Maybe we cannot understand everything here. After all, we are only human; we are not God. Is it any wonder that we sinful, puny humans do not understand everything about God? Are not His ways higher than our ways and His thoughts above our thoughts as the infinite heavens are higher than the earth?

Paul even goes on to state God's unconditional choice in another way by quoting the Old Testament. "I will have mercy on whom I have mercy, and I will have compassion on whom I have compassion" (9:15). And later on he says, "He has mercy on whom he wants, and whom he wants he hardens" (9:18). According to the Bible, the choice is entirely up to God. He is free to love whom He wants and to pass others by, not because of any good or bad in man, but for His own good reasons.

It would be possible for us to rest our evidence at any one of the numerous points mentioned above in Romans 9. Paul has demonstrated conclusively that salvation is not of him that works but of Him that calls, and that election is unconditional. There is no need to go on. And yet it almost seems as if Paul had the Arminians in mind when he wrote verse 16. For Paul says so unequivocally that there can be no misunderstanding at all, "So then it does not depend on the man who wills or the man who runs, but on God who has mercy" (New American Standard Version). The "it" refers to salvation. Could anything be clearer? Salvation does not depend on the man who wills, wants, or decides; nor on him who runs. It depends solely on God who has mercy.

If there is still anyone who doubts these explicit assertions of the Bible that our salvation is entirely in God's hands, and that it does not depend one whit on him who wills, or him who runs, then let him read and reread again and again Romans 9:16. For this is God's Word.

III. SOME CLARIFICATIONS

A. Has the Arminian escaped the problem?

One of the reasons the Arminian chooses to make man rather than God the decisive factor in his salvation is that he hopes to save man's freedom. He believes that if God foreordains all things, then man is not free and responsible. So he opts to reduce God's determinative plans and have a certain area where man acts freely and independently of God. (By way of anticipation, it should be noted that the Calvinist keeps both God's sovereignty and man's responsibility, even though he cannot rationally reconcile the two. See chapter 6.)

But it should be noted that the Arminian does not succeed very well in his goal. For according to the Arminian's own position, God foreknows all events. God did not choose who should believe on Christ; but God has known from all eternity what each man's choice would be, for God is omniscient. If, then, God foreknows what will come to pass in every event, then only that which He foreknows can come to pass. There can be no alternative. If God foreknew that Mr. A. would believe, then there is no possibility whatsoever of Mr. A's not believing. Thus if God does foreknow all things, as the Arminian says, then all things are certain to come to pass, and there is no possibility of an alternative.

Well, this is just exactly what the Calvinist believes: God foreknows all things, future events are certain, and man has a responsibility to do the right. The only difference is that the Calvinist dares to say that God is all-powerful and controls these events; whereas the Arminian says that man controls them. The Calvinist dares to make God a real God, an almighty God, and not a partially mighty God. And the Arminian has gained nothing by his theory, since he has exactly the same problem that the Calvinist has; namely, how to reconcile human responsibility with the absolute certainty of all events.

B. Man is free

Contrary to what most people think, the Calvinist teaches that man is free — one hundred percent free — free to do exactly what he wants. God does not coerce a single one against his will.

And just because man is free, man is a slave. Just because man does what he wants to do, man has no free will (which is different from saying that he is free); that is, man is totally unable to choose equally as well between the good and the bad. A compulsive drinker — an alcoholic — is not free. Technically he has the external choice of drinking or not drinking. But really there is only one thing he can do. He can no more stop drinking than he can stop breathing. He has to drink. He is a slave to alcohol. And yet he is free. He does exactly what he wants to do. Nobody is compelling him to drink.

In the same way, the non-Christian is free. He does precisely what he would like. He follows his heart's desires. Because his heart is rotten and inclined to all kinds of evil, he freely does what he wants to do, namely, sin. He hates the Triune God, and all He stands for. Therefore, in reality, he will never choose Him. He cannot, for he does not want to. Thus just because the unregenerate is free, he is a slave. He is a slave to the devil and his own evil desires, and cannot serve God.

Historically, the term *free agency* has been used in theology to designate that a man is free to do what he wants to do; and *free will* has been used to indicate the kind of freedom that no man has — namely, the ability or freedom to choose either good or evil, either to believe on Christ or to reject Him.

Incidentally, the Christian has no free will either.[3] He may technically have the external option to choose or reject Christ, but basically he does not. Christ will not let him reject Him. All that the Father has given to Christ will come to Christ. No one will snatch them out of Christ's hands (John 6:37, 39). In other words, the Christian does not have free will. So, if you are a real Christian, thank God that you will never for a moment be able to be a turncoat to Jesus. Calvinism is not so horrible after all, is it?

C. In predestination everybody gets what he wants

Sometimes people complain that predestination is a harsh doctrine that forces people to do what they do not want to do. They say that if they wanted to believe, they could not unless God had predestined them; and if they did not want to believe, God would drag them into heaven. So what is the use of believing?

Let it be firmly stated that everybody gets precisely what he wants. To put it in the most blunt way possible: hellians are glad they are in hell. Nobody is in hell against his will. Everyone there is glad that he is there. Do not misread that previous statement. Hellians know that after death everybody goes either to heaven or to hell. They do not like hell, otherwise it would not be hell. It is the place where the worm never dies and where

---

[3]Neither does God have free will. God cannot choose to do evil, because He is only good.

the fire is never quenched. In hell there is only agony always. It is hellish. So hellians do not like being there. But what they hate worse than their agony is God the Father, God the Son, and God the Holy Spirit. The last place they want to be is in heaven. They cannot stomach the idea of repenting for sins and loving God and others more than themselves. They do not want to be in hell, but when they know that the alternative to hell is to go to heaven with a pure heart, they would much rather stay in hell. So it is true that everyone gets what he wants: Christians are glad they are with God, and hellians are glad they are not with God.

Whenever a non-Christian complains about the teaching of predestination, it is usually a hypocritical rationalization for rejecting Christ. I would ask anybody: What do you want? Are you sorry for your sins? Do you trust in Christ as your Savior? Do you love God and want to go to heaven? If the reply is yes, then you should know that you are already a Christian. You have already believed. And "him that comes to me I will not drive away," says Jesus. You have what you want.

If you say no to those questions, then I would ask, "Why do you complain? You have what you want. You do not want to repent, you do not want Christ, you do not want heaven. Well, you have exactly what you want."

IV. PRACTICAL ADVANTAGES

These Biblical teachings about election are hard to understand. If someone still is in doubt about them, he should remember that salvation does not depend on believing all the Bible says about unconditional election. We can be confused in our thinking and even deny some Biblical truths, and yet be saved. Salvation does not depend on our having a theologian's knowledge. It depends only on whether or not we truly put our trust in Jesus Christ to save us from our sins. Therefore, both Arminians and Calvinists who repent of their sins and turn to Christ for salvation are going to be in heaven.

But if I were an Arminian, I would want to know with certainty what the Bible does say about election; for it is undeniable that the Arminian is losing out on much of the richness of the Christian life because of his views. Consider how this is so in two ways:

A. Praise and thanks to God

If you believe that Christ died for your sins and that you by the partial assistance of the Holy Spirit came to this assurance, you will be extremely grateful to God. But suppose, in addition to being grateful to Christ for dying on the cross for you, you realized that you would never have loved Jesus unless He first loved you, that you would never have chosen Him unless He had first chosen you and by the Holy Spirit had given you your faith in Him. Then you would love Him all the more. Your humility would be greater because you know that you are not even good enough to see a good thing when it is in front of you. Your thanks would be greater for you have more for which to be thankful. Your determination to live a better life would be greater because you have more for which to be thankful. How good God is not only to forgive us for our sins but also to give us faith in Christ so that we can have the forgiveness of sins. How good God is!

B. Assurance of salvation

If in the last analysis our salvation depends upon our free will to accept Christ, and if God provides the substitutionary atonement of Christ but not our faith, then we are in a miserable situation. Think of it — whether we stay Christians or not depends on us! What a frightful thought! Salvation depends on us, who by nature are rotten and do not love God? On us, who as Christians have the old man still within us? On us, who doubt, waver, and sin? Salvation depends on us? Oh, no, do not let that be. I believe today, but maybe I will not tomorrow. Maybe I will succumb to those sinful desires rather than be true to Christ. Maybe my skeptical professors will convince me that the Bible is not right. Such can be the agitations of one who thinks that in the final analysis his faith depends fundamentally on himself and has not been given him by God.

But the Calvinist knows that all of his salvation depends on God and not himself. He knows that not only did Christ die for his sins, but also that God gave him his faith. He knows that He who began a good work in him will continue this work until the day of judgment (Phil. 1:6). Thus the Arminian misses out on the joy and comfort of salvation because he places the confidence of his faith in himself rather than in God.

Praise God, from whom all blessings flow, including our faith, which is the means of securing the blessings of Christ's atonement. Praise Him for His electing love.

DISCUSSION QUESTIONS

1. Read what the Biblically based creeds say about election:
   a. The Belgic Confession (XVI). (See pp. 98-100.)
   b. The Westminster Confession (III). (See pp. 101-108.)
   c. The Canons of Dort (I). (See the back of the *Psalter Hymnal* of the Christian Reformed Church.)
   d. The Heidelberg Catechism (Question 54).
2. What is the difference between an Armenian and an Arminian?
3. What is the difference between predestination and foreordination?
4. What is the difference between predestination and fatalism?
5. What are the two parts of predestination?
6. What other words could be used for *election* and *electing*? See Ephesians 1:4, for example.
7. What is meant by the word *unconditional* in the term *unconditional election*?
8. What does Deuteronomy 7:6-9 say about the *unconditional* aspect of election?
9. Discuss Romans 8:29-30 thoroughly. Show from the rest of the Bible what "know" often means (cf. Gen. 4:1; 18:19; Num. 31:18; Ps. 1:6; Amos 3:2; Matt. 7:23; I Cor. 8:3; II Tim. 2:19).
10. Study Romans 9:10-26, and especially verses 11, 14, 16, and 19. What do these verses have to say about election?
11. How does I John 4:19 affect the teaching of election?
12. In what sense is it Biblical to say that, although God predestinates everyone, man is free?
13. Does the Arminian solve the problem of how to reconcile human responsibility with the foreordination and certainty of all events? Explain.
14. How are you going to answer someone who says, "If I am predestinated to be saved, I will be saved any way. So I'll sin all I want"?
15. Or what would you say if he said, "If I am not predestinated to be saved, I can't be saved. So I won't even try to be saved. I can't do anything about it"?
16. How would you answer a person who says, "If unconditional election is true, then God is arbitrary, a respecter of person, who chooses some and is hardhearted to others"?
17. Is it possible for someone to make sure he is elected? How? See the Canons of Dort (I, 12).
18. Would God have been unfair if He did not elect anybody but let all mankind go to hell? See the Canons of Dort (I, 1; III–IV, 15).
19. If someone refuses to accept Christ, whose fault is it: God's for not electing him? or that person's? How would you prove that from the Bible?
20. Be very honest now. Do you like the teaching of election? Why?

21. How does the teaching of election make a Calvinist praise God more than an Arminian does?
22. How can you "make your calling and election sure" (II Peter 1:10)?
23. You can know if someone is elected. How? But can you know if he is reprobate? Why?
24. How does the teaching of election help to give you the assurance of salvation?
25. Should we talk about election with children? with non-Christians? with adult Christians? Why?
26. Judging by numbers, it seems that people like the doctrine of Arminianism more than Calvinism. Why is this so?

3
limited atonement

I. THE PROBLEM

For whom did Christ intend to die? Whose sins did Christ actually pay for? For whom did Christ go to hell? Whom did Christ reconcile to God? For whom was Christ a substitute? What was His intent, His purpose, in dying? To save everyone or only those whom God elected? For a long time orthodox Christians have answered these questions in two different ways. The Arminian has said, "Christ died for everyone"; whereas the Calvinist has said, "Christ died for only the believer." The Arminian has taught universal atonement; whereas the Calvinist has taught limited atonement.

The Arminian says that Christ died for all the world, including Esau and Judas. Christ, they say, paid for the sins of even the reprobate, those who consciously reject Jesus, those who go to hell. They make a disjunction between what Christ did (He died for all) and what Christ accomplished (all are not saved). To them the atonement is like a universal grab-bag: there is a package for everyone, but only some will grab a package. Christ not only shed His blood, He also spilled it. He intended to save all, but only some will be saved. Therefore, some of His blood was wasted: it was spilled.

An illustration of the Arminian position may be found in the case of an American who more than a hundred years ago was sentenced to be hanged. Before the time of his execution, however, President Andrew Jackson granted him a pardon. But the man refused and even appealed to the Supreme Court, which upheld his right to refuse a pardon. The Court declared that the president may grant a pardon, but that a pardon may never be

forced on a person, and may be rejected. Similarly, the Arminian says, God may offer man a pardon on the basis of Christ's
death, but a condemned sinner may reject that pardon. However, anyone who would reject a pardon — from God or from the
president — is a fool.

To bolster his position, the Arminian appeals to such passages
as I John 2:2 ("he is the propitiation for our sins; and not for ours
only, but also for the whole world"), II Corinthians 5:14 ("the
love of Christ constrains us, because we judge that one died for
all"), and John 4:42 ("this is indeed the Savior of the world").

The Calvinist, on the other hand, says that Christ died only
for the believer, the elect, only for those who will actually be
saved and go to heaven. According to the Calvinist, Christ
intended or purposed that His atonement should pay for the sins
of only those the Father had given Him (John 6:37-40). He says
that if Christ actually took away the penalty of everybody's
sins, then everybody is saved. But such a conclusion is obviously
not true. People do go to hell. The Calvinist appeals to those
passages that state that Christ died, not for everyone, but for
"his people" (Matt. 1:21), His "sheep" (John 10:15; cf. 10:26),
"his friends" (John 15:13), "the church" (Acts 20:28), and "the
bride" (Eph. 5:25).

When the Calvinist uses the term *limited,* he does not mean
that the atonement is limited in its power to save. On the contrary, he believes that the atonement of Christ is unlimited in its
power, that Christ saves to the "uttermost," and that the atonement is of infinite worth and value. But he does believe that
the unlimited atonement of Christ is limited in its scope, that
Christ intended to and actually did remove the guilt of the sins
of a limited number of people — namely, those whom God has
loved with a special love from eternity. The atonement of unlimited value is limited to certain people. It is an unlimited
atonement.

Because the term *limited atonement* may confuse people,
some have preferred the terms *definite* or *particular* instead.
These latter terms emphasize the objects of the atonement.
They stress that the atonement, which is unlimited in its power,
is limited to a definite, particular number of people, namely, the
believers. It makes no difference whether one uses the term
limited or *definite* or *particular,* as long as these distinctions are
kept in mind.

II. THE BIBLICAL ANSWER

Before going to major Biblical data, observe two passages that deal with limited atonement: John 10:15 and Ephesians 5:25.

In John 10 Jesus uses the illustration of the shepherd and his flock. He says that He is a shepherd and that He has a flock of sheep. He knows them and they know Him. They hear His voice and follow after Him, and He gives to them eternal life so that they will never perish. These sheep are the true believers. Now it is for these sheep and not for the whole world that Jesus says He lays down His life: "The good shepherd lays down his life for the sheep" (10:11). And in 10:15 He says again, "I lay down my life for the sheep." This is limited atonement. He lays down His life for His sheep, and His sheep alone. In 10:26 He tells those who do not believe in Him that they are not of His sheep. "But you believe not," He says to the unbelieving Jews, "because you are not of my sheep." In other words, they were not included in His flock, for whom, He had said earlier, He would lay down His life. That is limited atonement.

In Ephesians 5:25-27 Paul admonishes husbands in the Ephesian church to love their wives "even as Christ also loved the church and gave himself up for it." It is the church, not the world, for whom Christ gave Himself up.

Furthermore, He gave Himself up for it to "sanctify it, having cleansed it." There is an inseparable unity between Christ's death for the church and His sanctifying and cleansing it. Those for whom He died He also sanctifies and cleanses. Since the world is not sanctified and cleansed, then it is obvious that Christ did not die for it.

Moreover, if the Arminian view was correct that Christ loved the whole world equally and gave Himself up for the world, then the parallel between the bride of the husband and the bride of Christ would fall. For then the injunction would be that a husband should love and give himself up for other than his wife, just as Christ gave Himself up not only for the church — His bride — but also for those outside it. But this would be contradictory to Scripture, which teaches that a man should have one wife.

Now let us look at the Biblical basis for limited atonement from the standpoint of the Father, the Son, and the Holy Spirit, and see the unity and harmony of their purpose and work.

A. The Father's election

If the Arminian is correct in his denial of election; if God did not predestinate some to life eternal, but postdestinated them; if God has not loved certain people with a particular love from eternity; if God was not determined from eternity to save His people and them alone – then there is no limited atonement but a universal one. The two go together: an indefinite love and an indefinite atonement, a universal love and a universal atonement, an indiscriminate love and an indiscriminate atonement, and an unlimited election (God elects everybody) and an unlimited atonement. If God has not loved certain people with a particular love, then the Arminian is right: God did not send His Son to die for any particular ones. If God has loved all people alike, then God has indeed sent His Son to die for *all* people alike. The Arminian is correct in observing that the Father's love and the Son's atonement go together, that the same people are in view in both God's love and His atonement, that there is a unity between the Father's love and the Son's death. The objects of both are the same. The Arminian and the Calvinist agree at this point.

But the Bible teaches again and again that God does not love all people with the same love. "You only have I loved of all the families of the earth" (Amos 3:2); "Those whom God foreloved, he also foreordained" (Rom. 8:29); "Jacob I loved, but Esau I hated" (Rom. 9:13). See again chapter 2, "Unconditional Election." The term "loved by God" is not applied to the world, but only to the saints at Rome (1:7), Colossae (3:12), and Thessalonica (I Thess. 1:4; II Thess. 2:13), and to the Christian addressees of Jude (v. 1).

Since the objects of the Father's love are particular, definite, and limited, so are the objects of Christ's death. Because God has loved certain ones and not all, because He has sovereignly and immutably determined that these particular ones will be saved, He sent His Son to die for them, to save them, and not all the world. Because there is a definite election, there is a definite atonement. Because there is a limited election, there is a limited atonement. Because there is a particular election, there is a particular atonement. God's electing love and Christ's atonement go hand in hand and have the same people in view. There is unity between the Father and the Son.

It was just because God so loved the world of elect sinners

that He sent His only begotten Son that the world might be saved through Him (John 3:16-17). In this passage "world" does not mean every single person, reprobate as well as elect, but the whole world in the sense of people from every tribe and nation — not only the Jews.[1]

It was just because the Father had given some people to Jesus that Jesus came to earth to die for them (John 6:37-40). Jesus had a definite, precise goal in mind, one which coincided with the Father's purpose. His purpose was not to die indefinitely for everybody in the world as He said, but that "all that the Father gives me will come to me" (v. 37). The decretive will of the Father was not that all should be saved but that Jesus should not lose a single one that the Father gave Him (v. 39). For this purpose alone Jesus died (v. 38).

I John 4:10 is also clear in teaching an inseparable relationship between the love of God and the atonement of Christ, for it says that God "loved us and sent his Son to be a propitiation for our sins." The object of God's love is the same as the object of Christ's propitiation. The "us" refers not to the world but to those whose sins are forgiven (2:12), who have overcome the evil one (2:13), and who are children of God (3:1, 2). In other words, Christ died only for the children of God: those whom God loved with a special love.

Paul also identifies the people for whom Christ died with the people whom God loves when he writes: "But God commends his love for us in that while we were yet sinners Christ died for us" (Rom. 5:8). The object of God's love ("us") is the same as those for whom Christ died ("us"). Because of God's distinguishing love for "us" — the saints (1:7) and the justified (5:1) — Christ died for the same.

Perhaps the most forceful passage of all that shows the intimate and necessary relationship between limited election and limited atonement is Romans 8:32. This verse is all the more striking because it is one to which the unlimited atonement theorists constantly appeal. It reads: "He who spared not his own Son but delivered him up for us all, will he not also with him freely give us all things?" At first blush, it may seem that Paul is clearly teaching that Christ died for all. But on more matured reflection it becomes clear that this is impossible.

---

[1]William Hendriksen summarizes six different ways the word *world* is used in the Gospel of John alone. See his commentary on John at 1:10.

The "all" of verse 32 refers to all the elect, and not to every single person in the whole world. The reason for saying this is that the entire passage of Romans 8:28 to the end of the chapter deals with only Christians. Everything immediately before and immediately after verse 32 refers only to God's special people. All things do not work together for good for the whole world, but only for those who love God and who are called according to His electing purpose (v. 28). God's promises are only for those whom He has foreknown and foreordained and justified and glorified (vv. 29-30). It is of these people that Paul says, "If God is for us, who can be against us? He that spared not his own Son, but delivered him up for us all, how shall he not also with him freely give us all things?" (v. 32). The "us all," for whom Christ died, are those Christians Paul has just mentioned.

Then, in the very next sentence, Paul continues to speak of only the elect: "Who will lay anything to the charge of God's elect?" The idea is: nobody can, because Christ died for them. See the close connection between the elect and those for whom Christ died? They are the same. Everything that precedes and follows the "us all" in verse 32 is restricted to the elect, to those loved by God. Therefore this verse, instead of supporting a universalistic atonement, does the precise opposite: it limits the "us all" to those who love God. That is limited atonement.

Incidentally, it is just this limited atonement that gives such a real comfort in time of trouble. For Paul reasons (v. 32) that if God gave the biggest thing in the world for His people — that is, if God sacrificed His Son Jesus for us who believe — then He will give us every other thing that is good for us. So, you don't have to worry, you of little faith, you who are so fearful about tomorrow. Remember, if He sacrificed Christ for you, then everything else that is good for you is a trifle. And God will give it to you. Thank God the Father not only for His eternal, electing love, but also thank God the Son for dying for you.

To sum up this section, the Bible teaches that the purpose of the Father's predestination and the Son's atonement is the same: the salvation of a limited number of people, God's elect. In other words, limited atonement is based on unconditional election.

B. The Son's atonement

To answer the question: For whom did Christ die? it is necessary to define the word *die*. What is meant by *die*? Just exactly what did Jesus do when He died? Here is the heart of the question.

The Bible defines the death of Jesus in at least four different ways. When Christ died, (1) He made a substitutionary sacrifice for sins (Heb. 9, 10); (2) He propitiated, that is, appeased or placated, the righteous wrath of God (Rom. 3:25; Heb. 2:17; I John 2:2; 4:10); (3) He reconciled His people to God — that is, He removed the enmity between them and God (Rom. 5:10; II Cor. 5:20; etc.); and (4) He redeemed them from the curse of the law (Gal. 3:13).

The question that needs a precise answer is this: Did He or didn't He? Did Christ actually make a substitutionary sacrifice for sins or didn't He? If He did, then it was not for all the world, for then all the world would be saved.

Did Christ actually — not theoretically, not on paper, but really — redeem Judas from the curse of the law by actually becoming a curse for him (Gal. 3:13), so that Judas is no longer under the curse of the law? Of course not. Paul says that Christ was made a curse for us, that is, Paul and the believing Galatians. Because Judas would not believe on Christ, he is in hell under the curse of the law. Christ did not die for him.

Did Christ truly, actually, really reconcile Esau to the Father by His death (Rom. 5:10), or didn't He? Did He by His substitutionary death actually remove the enmity so that God is no longer alienated from Esau, or didn't He?

It is one or the other. If Christ did reconcile Esau, if He did become a curse for Judas, if He actually endured the torments of hell for all men — in other words, if He died for all — then no one is lost. All are reconciled and redeemed. But to say that all men are redeemed is contradictory to the Bible.

Thus the nature of the atonement — what did Christ actually do? — answers the question: For whom did Christ die? The noun (*atonement*) defines its adjective (*limited*). If the atonement does not actually save, does not really remove God's curse from people, does not actually redeem them, then it indeed can be for all the world, even for those who are in hell. But if the death of Jesus is what the Bible says it is — a substitutionary sacrifice for sins, an actual and not a hypothetical redemption, whereby the sinner is really reconciled to God — then, obviously, it cannot be for every man in the world. For then everybody would be saved, and obviously they are not.

One of two things is true: either the atonement is limited in its extent or it is limited in its nature or power. It cannot be unlimited in both. If it is unlimited in its extent — that is, that Christ died for every single person, as the Arminian claims — then it cannot be unlimited in its nature, in its power; for then all would be saved. Because the Arminian believes in an atonement that is unlimited in extent, it is necessarily a vague, indefinite, poverty stricken atonement that does not actually save anyone. If, on the other hand, the atonement is unlimited as to its efficacy, its saving power, as the Bible indicates, then it must be limited in its scope. Unless a person believes in universalism — that all people will be saved — the atonement cannot be unlimited in both its nature and its extent. Therefore, it is Biblical to speak of an unlimited (as to nature and power) limited (as to its extent) atonement. Or, an unlimited, definite, particular atonement.

When it is realized that the atonement is real and not fictive, that it actually and not imaginarily took away the guilt of sins, then it is possible to see the error in the illustration of the prisoner condemned to be hanged, but who was pardoned by President Jackson. The reason the illustration fails and the man could refuse the pardon was that the pardon had no objective basis. If another man had been hanged in his place — if another man had paid the debt — then the state could not have exacted two penalties for the same deed. But there was no such substitute for that man. In the case of the atonement, however, there is not a mere fictive pardon without a real substitute; for Christ really died in the place of sinners. He made an actual sacrifice for sins. God punished Christ instead of His loved ones. But nobody was a substitute in the pardoning of the hanged man. If he had accepted the pardon, then the strict and just demands of the law would have been overlooked. But this is something that cannot happen with divine law. Someone has to die to pay for sins committed: either the person himself or else Christ.

C. The Spirit's indwelling

II Corinthians 5:14-15 tells us that "Christ's love constrains us, for we judge that if one died for all, therefore all died; and that he died for all that they who live might henceforth live not unto themselves, but unto him who died and rose again for their sakes." This is another striking example of how a text may seem at first glance to support a universalistic theory of the atonement but in reality does just the opposite. Often Paul's phrase "one died for all" is appealed to as evidence of unlimited atonement — that Christ died for every single individual that ever lived or ever shall live. Yet a careful study of the passage reveals that Paul teaches the contrary.

Note, in particular, the "therefore." Paul writes that "one died for all, therefore all died." Because of the death of Christ, Paul says, all died. There is an inseparable connection between the death of Christ and the death of all. The "therefore" demands a causal relationship. Hence, the "all died" cannot refer to the natural death of all men, for Christ's death is not the cause of man's physical death. The "all died" refers to the spiritual death of the believer. It is the same sort of death of Romans 6, where Paul says that Christians are baptized into, or united to, the death of Christ. They have died to sin through the working of the Holy Spirit in their hearts. Now it is obvious that all people have not died in this sense. Many people are living in sin; they have not died to sin. Therefore Christ could not have died for them. For there is that unbreakable relationship between the death of Christ and those for whom He died: "He died for all. Therefore, all died." Obviously, the *all* in both cases means all the believers — not all the world, reprobate as well as elect. For the reprobate never died to sin.

Furthermore, Paul goes on to note, in line with Romans 6, that if Christians are dead to sins, then they are made alive in Christ. If they are spiritually buried with Christ, they will spiritually rise with Him. (Although Paul does not state it explicitly in this passage, we know from the rest of Scripture that this is possible only through the Holy Spirit's working.) Then he goes one step further and reasons that Christ's love toward Christians should constrain them to live godly lives, all for the sake of "him who for their sakes died and rose again."

In other words, there is an inexorable chain of events in II Corinthians 5:14-15: (a) Christ died for all believers; therefore, (b) all believers die spiritually in Christ; and (c) they all rise again spiritually in Christ. If (a) is stated, (b) and (c) must follow. So in this passage there is no mention of the world, the unbeliever, but only of those who died to sin, rose spiritually in Christ, and live for Him. Thus the "all" of "one died for all" refers to all Christians. That is limited atonement.

❊   ❊   ❊

This then is the grand scheme of redemption. God did not vaguely love all men without sovereignly electing them. And then Christ did not indefinitely die for all men — hypothetically, not actually taking away their sin. And the Holy Spirit did not insipidly apply the death of Christ to all, leaving it in their hands ultimately as to whether or not they would be saved.

But, rather, the Bible teaches a unity in the work of the three Persons of the Trinity: between the Father's election, the Son's atonement, and the Spirit's indwelling. Because the Father has loved certain ones from eternity (Rom. 8:29), He sent His Son to die for them. Lovingly, the Son lost none the Father gave Him (John 6:39), but became a curse for His sheep, His people, His church, His bride. He actually saved them, redeemed them, and reconciled them to the Father. Then, the Spirit came to these people whom the Father had chosen and for whom the Son had died and He caused them to die to sin and to be spiritually alive, that is, to be born again. The purpose of the Father, Son, and Holy Spirit coincide. They strive for and accomplish the same purpose: the salvation of those whom the Father has loved with a special love.[2]

III. THE OBJECTIONS

Traditionally there have arisen certain objections to the Biblical doctrine of limited atonement. It may be helpful to consider at least three of these.

A. The free offer of the gospel

Some say, if Christ did not take away the sins of all, if the Father, Son, and Holy Spirit did not intend to save all — then

---

[2]Some have attempted to keep election and the sovereign working of the Holy Spirit, but at the same time deny limited atonement. Such a theory drives an unbiblical disjunction between the work of the Father, Son, and Spirit. It pictures the Father as loving all men alike, the Son as dying for all men alike, but the Holy Spirit as working irresistibly in the hearts of only certain people. How much better it is to stick to the Biblical data which portray complete unity between all the Persons of the Trinity for the securing of the one purpose: the fulfillment of the Father's election.

For an excellent Biblical discussion of this problem, as well as the whole teaching of limited atonement, see the report in the 1967 *Acts of Synod* of the Christian Reformed Church (pp. 514-607). This is no ivory tower study, but one that grew out of a practical situation.

how is it possible to say, as the Calvinist does, that God sincerely offers salvation to all, including those whom He has not fore-ordained to be saved?

Here we stand before a fundamental mystery. On the one hand, the Bible teaches that God intends that salvation will be for only certain people. On the other hand, the Bible unequivocally declares that God freely and sincerely offers salvation to everyone.

Ezekiel says, for example, "Say unto them, As I live, says Jehovah, I have no pleasure in the death of the wicked; but that the wicked turn from his way and live. Turn you, turn you from your evil ways; for why will you die, O house of Israel?" (33:11).

Isaiah says, "Ho, everyone that thirsts, come to the waters; and he who has no money, come, buy and eat" (55:1). Elsewhere he says, "Look unto me, and be ye saved, all the ends of the earth" (45:22).

Jesus says, "Come unto me, all you who labor and are heavy laden, and I will give you rest" (Matt. 11:28). Later, He exclaims: "O Jerusalem, Jerusalem, who kills the prophets, and stones those who were sent to you. How often I would have gathered your children together as a hen gathers her chicks under her wings, and you would not" (Matt. 23:37).

Peter writes with unmistakable clarity that the Lord is "long-suffering toward you, not wishing that any should perish, but that all should come to repentance" (II Peter 3:9).

Finally, in Revelation 22:17 we read that universal invitation: "And the Spirit and the bride say, Come. And he who hears, let him say, Come. And he who is thirsty, let him come. He who will, let him take the water of life freely."

How is it possible to reconcile these two sets of statements: on the one hand, God intends to save only certain ones; and, on the other hand, God sincerely offers salvation to all? Do not all the passages which were just quoted prove that Christ did die for all? For if He sincerely offers salvation to all, He must have made provision for their salvation.

Here we come again to that fundamental problem of God. His ways are higher than our ways, and His thoughts than our thoughts. To man it seems impossible to reconcile both truths. They seem to contradict each other. Yet, the Bible is the infallible Word of God and cannot err. Since both sets of truths are in the Bible, they must be accepted; and man must resign himself to the fact that he cannot understand God and His ways.

He must be humble enough to recognize that the creature cannot comprehend God's thoughts. He must simply ask: Did God make these two statements which are seemingly contradictory? If he finds them both to be in the Bible, as the Calvinist does, then he must accept them. He must not say that he will accept only that which his finite mind can understand. For then he automatically rules out the possibility of God, for God is infinitely greater than his mind and is incomprehensible.

B. Universalistic passages

An objection to limited atonement is sometimes made on the fact that the Bible explicitly says in several passages that Christ is the propitiation for the sins of the whole world (I John 2:2), that He is the Savior of the world (John 4:42), that He takes away the sin of the world (John 1:29), that "he died for all" (II Cor. 5:14-15), and that He gave Himself a ransom for all (I Tim. 2:6). If He died for all, it is reasoned, then He did not die for a limited number.

The answer to this objection is that often the Bible uses the words *world* or *all* in a restricted, limited sense. They must always be interpreted in their context and in the light of the rest of Scripture. We must do this in any normal reading. For example, if a newspaper should report that a ship was sunk, but all were rescued, it is obvious that it means that all that were on the ship were rescued, and not all that are in the world.

The same is true in the Bible. When Luke records that Caesar commanded that "all the world" should be enrolled and that "all went to enroll themselves, every one to his own city" (2:1, 2), it is clear that *all* is not *all*. For the Japanese, Chinese, and Anglo-Saxons did not enroll themselves.

When Paul twice asserts that "all things are lawful" for him (I Cor. 6:12; 10:23), it is obvious from the rest of his writings that all things are not lawful for him. It is not lawful for him to sin.

When Jesus says: "And I, when I am lifted up from the earth, will draw all men to myself" (John 12:32), it is plain that *all* is not *all*. For millions of heathen have not even heard of Jesus, let alone been drawn to Him. And many other millions who have heard of Jesus, rather than having been attracted by Him, have been repelled at the very thought of Him. Jesus may have meant one of two things: all the elect would be drawn to Him, or all kinds of men — Gentiles as well as Jews, Hottentots as well as Swedes — would be drawn to Him. But one thing is clear: all men have not been drawn to Him. *All* is not *all*.

Similarly, in I Corinthians 15:22 Paul writes in seemingly universal terms when he says: "As in Adam all died, so also in Christ all will be made alive." Although it is clear that every person in the world died in Adam (Rom. 5:12 ff.), it is equally clear that everybody has not died in Christ. There are many people who have not been crucified in Christ. They hate Him.

In the light of so many passages (and these could be increased) where *all* does not mean *all* in the sense of every individual that lives, it is impossible to make an offhand appeal to these universalistic passages to prove that Christ died for everybody. The context must be carefully studied. When we did that with Romans 8:32 and II Corinthians 5:14-15, it was clear from the context that Paul was asserting that Christ died for all the elect. In the other places the words *world* and *all* simply refer to all the believers, the whole church, and the international world far beyond Israel. In I John 2:2, for example, we read that Christ "is the propitiation for our sins; and not for ours only, but also for the whole world." This means that Christ died for the sins not only of Jews, but also of Dutchmen, Italians, and Swedes — in fact, for the whole world. It does not mean for every single Jew, Dutchman, Italian, and Swede.

C. A hindrance to evangelism

Some reason that if an evangelist cannot say to his audience, "Christ died for you," his effectiveness in winning souls will be measurably hurt.

The answer to such reasoning is that, if there has to be a choice, it is better to tell the truth and not to win so many converts than to win many by a falsehood. The end does not justify an illegitimate means. If the Bible says that Christ died for the elect, then an evangelist may not play God by stating that he knows that everyone in his audience is elect and, therefore, that Christ died for them. He does not know and should not state it.

But it should also be noted that the effectiveness of evangelism does not depend on the unbiblical statement "Christ died for you." You will never find such a statement in George Whitefield or Charles Spurgeon, for example, and yet their evangelistic success was phenomenal. It is noteworthy that nowhere in the Bible is such an expression to be found. It is sufficient simply to say to an unconverted person: "Christ died for sin. He gave Himself for sinners just like you and me. If you want to be saved, believe on Him. It is your responsibility, and God freely offers you salvation through Jesus. Believe."[3] Such a statement is Biblical and very effective. The great Baptist, Charles Haddon Spurgeon, is an excellent example of how effective a preacher can be who does not tone down the Biblical teachings of Calvinism.

Moreover, limited atonement, instead of being a hindrance to evangelism, is a great encouragement to it. For if we believe with the Bible that by nature everyone is depraved, and yet that God has His people in every nation, in every tribe, and in every community, and that Christ has taken away the sins of these people, then how encouraging it is to preach the gospel. It isn't hopeless after all. There will be success. All we have to do is to do our duty and tell others about Christ. And because the atonement of Christ has actually taken away the sins of the elect, there will be an infallible response on their part. People from every tribe and tongue will believe, because Christ died for them.

DISCUSSION QUESTIONS

1. Read what the Canons of Dort say about limited atonement (II).
2. State precisely what limited atonement means.
   a. What is atonement?
   b. Why is it called *limited*?
3. How can the word *limited* in the term *limited atonement* be misleading?
4. In what sense is the atonement limited? In what sense is it unlimited?
5. Is *definite atonement* any better? Why?
6. Is *particular atonement* any better? Why?

---

[3]It is certainly possible when speaking to the unsaved to say in one sense that "Christ died for you." Because of the death of Christ, many blessings flow to the reprobate: all the natural blessings of this world come through the mediatorial dominion of Christ. But all these blessings are nonsalvational: they do not terminate in the redemption of the person. Therefore, although technically speaking, it is proper to say to the unbeliever, "Christ died for you," such a statement is more than likely to be very misleading and should only be used when it is properly understood. The average person, upon hearing that Christ died for him, would conclude first of all that Christ took away the guilt of his sins. This may not be the case, and so it is better not to state dogmatically what may be wrong.

7. What is the Arminian position in regard to this teaching?
8. Why is the illustration concerning the hanged man under the presidency of Jackson not a good one?
9. How is limited atonement related to unconditional election?
10. Turn in your Bible to John 10:11, 15, and 16 to see what it says about for whom Christ died.
11. Turn to Romans 8:32. What does this say about limited atonement?
12. How can you prove limited atonement from the substitutionary atonement of Christ?
13. What would happen if the atonement were unlimited in extent and in power?
14. Cite as many passages as you can from both the Old and New Testaments to show that God offers salvation to all people without exception, the elect and the nonelect.
15. Read what the Canons of Dort say about the sincere offer of salvation (III–IV, 8).
16. And what did the Christian Reformed Church say in the 1924 *Acts of Synod?*
17. How do you reconcile the passages of question 14 with limited atonement?
18. Turn to the following verses in the Bible and explain how you reconcile these with the Biblical teaching of limited atonement:
    a. John 1:29
    b. John 4:42
    c. II Corinthians 5:14-15
    d. I Timothy 2:6
    e. I John 2:2
19. Is it Biblical to say to a non-Christian, "Christ died for you"?
20. How is limited atonement an encouragement to missionaries?
21. What comfort do you derive from the fact of limited atonement?

4

irresistible grace

Two college students attend a Bible study of Inter-Varsity Christian Fellowship. One says, "That's great"; the other says, "Poppycock." Two strangers hear a clear sermon on "I am the way, the truth, and the life; no one comes to the Father except through me." One believes; the other does not. Two boys — in fact, twins — are brought up in the same home with the same religious instruction. One loves God, and the other hates Him. Their names are Jacob and Esau.

Why? Why do two people in precisely the same circumstances react in opposite ways? Why does one person believe, and another reject Christ? That is the problem of this chapter.

The Biblical answer is irresistible grace. Irresistible grace is the sole cause for these different reactions.

I. WHAT IS IRRESISTIBLE GRACE?

A. Grace

Grace is undeserved favor.

A college student is more interested in trouble than in education. He disrupts the lecture of a distinguished visiting professor, thus depriving him of the right to speak and the other students of their right to listen. He even punches a paraplegic in the face as he attempts to go to class. He, with a gang, burns down the college library, cuts the hoses of the firemen, yells obscenities at the police, and even murders a fellow student who is the head of the opposing group. This thug is convicted in court of all these crimes and is sentenced to die. While in prison, he continues his hateful, revengeful tirades against those who work for peace, order, and freedom. But the state legislature grants him a complete pardon and even votes him a ten-thousand-dollar-a-year income for life. That is grace: unmerited favor.

In a similar fashion, everyone of us has committed much more heinous crimes — and these against God — and we deserve a much greater punishment. God made mankind good. But we willfully and freely rebelled against Him. He pleads with us to turn from sin and self to Him, and we answer Him by ridiculing Him. It is our nature to hate God with full vengeance, and to hate everyone else. Our one goal is to be the top man on the totem pole with God in the dirt. We deserve eternal hell fire.

It is in such a hateful situation as that, while we are still unrepentant sinners, that God loves certain ones, sends Jesus to die for them, and then sends His Holy Spirit to cause them to accept the sacrifice that Christ has made for them. To top it off, He ordains that those spiritual bastards (Heb. 12:8) will become His own children and that they will inherit unsearchable riches. Now that is undeserved favor. That is grace. (And it is open to whosoever will. If anyone wants it, he may put his trust in Christ right now, and take it. He may ask Christ, the God-man, to save him from his sins.)

B. Irresistible

Irresistible means that when God has chosen some to be saved and when He sends His Spirit to change them from being hateful to being loving, no one can resist Him. He is irresistible. He does what He sets out to do.

But do not misunderstand the word *irresistible*. To some it may give the meaning of causing someone to do what he does not want to do. An avalanche of snow may fall from a high mountain with an irresistible force, sweeping a villager to death when he obviously does not want to go. A Communist may force a preacher out of his pulpit and irresistibly put him in prison. A strong man may kidnap a three-year-old. The kidnaper cannot be resisted.

It is in this way that some conceive of irresistible grace. They picture God as forcing people to do what they do not want to do. He drags them struggling and kicking, as it were, into heaven against their wills. He forces, coerces, and does violence to man's will.

But this is not the meaning of the word *irresistible* in irresistible grace; and if it causes misunderstanding, then another word may be chosen. For example, *efficacious*, or *effectual*, or *unconquerable*, or *certain*. All that irresistible grace means is that God sends His Holy Spirit to work in the lives of people so that they will definitely and certainly be changed from evil to good people. It means that the Holy Spirit will certainly — without any and's, if's and but's — cause everyone whom God has chosen from eternity and for whom Christ died to believe on Jesus.

But God always does this in a way that man likes. As we said before, man is always free. He does exactly what he wants to do. This does not mean that he has free will — that is, the ability to choose the good and the bad equally as well. He does not have that kind of freedom. For he hates God, loves sin, and freely, willingly sins without any external compulsion. He is never able to choose the good, God, and Christ, because he is in slavery to the devil and his own sinful desires. He has no real freedom.

By nature man is like a person who loves to eat rotten, moldy, wormy apples out of the garbage can, or who likes to sit in the dirt and eat ashes. It is possible for God to change such a person's makeup so that he will love filet mignon and artichokes instead of ashes, and so that he will crave for a bowl of fresh fruit instead of a moldy apple.

In a similar way, God changes the heart of man from evil to good. By nature man loves sin and everything that is going to bring him unhappiness and eternal punishment. By irresistible grace God does not leave the heart unchanged and thus drag man into heaven against his will. No, God regenerates the man, changes his nature, and radically alters his character so that man now is truly sorry for his sin and loves God. Now, with his heart changed, he abhors the things he used to do. Now Christ is the fairest among ten thousand. Christianity now becomes exciting. He freely, eagerly seeks God.

This is how the irresistible, efficacious grace of God works.

C. Erroneous views

In order to make even clearer what irresistible grace is, it will be helpful to contrast this Biblical position with two erroneous views, Pelagianism and Semi-Pelagianism.

1. *Pelagianism*

Pelagianism is an old heresy — Pelagius lived in the fifth century — that is constantly with us under different names. It is the antithesis of Calvinism, or better still, of Augustinianism, since Augustine was mainly responsible for its defeat in the church. Augustinianism, or Calvinism, says that man is totally depraved and can do no good at all by himself and apart from the irresistible work of the Holy Spirit. Pelagianism, on the other hand, says that man is not depraved at all, neither totally nor partially. Rather, he is born perfectly good and can, with equal ability, choose the good or the bad. As a matter of fact, some are even sinless. Thus, according to Pelagianism, there is no need for the Holy Spirit or His irresistible grace to help man do good.

Such teaching is thoroughly pagan, and the Christian church soundly rejected it at the Synod of Carthage (418), the Council of Ephesus (431), and the Synod of Orange (529).

2. *Semi-Pelagianism*

In between Calvinism and Pelagianism is a mediating position, called Semi-Pelagianism or Arminianism. It did not like Pelagianism, because Pelagianism said that man could be sinless without the aid of the Holy Spirit. It did not like Augustinianism, because Augustinianism said that man is totally evil, unable to do a single good thing without the irresistible work of the Holy Spirit.

So the Semi-Pelagians wanted a compromise. They taught that man had some good in him, some ability to believe on Christ. To be sure, they said, natural man cannot believe without God's help: he needs the support of the Holy Spirit. But, says the Semi-Pelagian and Catholic[1] and Arminian, God does not give him this faith in an irresistible way. Cooperation is the byword. God does His part and man his part. They work together.

As one evangelist with this position says, "There is one area in your life that God will never touch — your will. He will never cause you to believe. That's your job. Only you can do it."

Or, as another writes, "We must repudiate the view that God regenerates man before he is convicted of sin, repents, converts, and believes. Such a view makes God arbitrarily determine the salvation or reprobation of individuals on no other principles than His own good pleasure or sovereign will. . . . Neither God

---

[1]The Dominicans, however, are close to the Calvinistic position. See, for example, Franz Diekamp, *Katholische Dogmatik*.

nor any one else is able to convert us if we do not convert." According to him, man must first of all repent and believe, and then God will regenerate man.

Return now to the question at the start of the chapter: Why does one person believe on Christ, whereas another in the same circumstances rejects? There are basically two answers: man's will or God's will. The Arminian, the Semi-Pelagian, and the Pelagian say that the difference between the two men is to be found in their own wills. God presents the gospel alike to those who reject and to those who accept. He comes with the preaching of the Word, the presentation of Christ, the offer of salvation. But He does not cause anyone to believe. Man is the ultimate deciding factor. If man does not accept Christ, then God cannot do anything about it.

The Calvinist, on the other hand, says that in the last instance the difference lies with God and not with man. In one man the Spirit is not working in a saving way. Therefore, because the man is spiritually dead, he cannot believe, even though he hears the external preaching of the Word and perhaps reads it for himself many times. In another man, however, the Holy Spirit works irresistibly, regenerating him so that he understands fully that he is a sinner and needs God, and, therefore, wants to believe and to be saved.

Thus according to the Arminian, the reason one accepts and another rejects the gospel is that *man* decides; but according to the Calvinist, it is that *God* decides. In the one case, faith is man's gift to God; in the other, it is God's gift to man. Hence we have two diametrically opposed answers to the question why some reject the gospel and others believe.

II. ITS SCRIPTURAL BASIS

The Five Points of Calvinism all depend on each other. If **T** is true, then **U** is true, and so are **L**, **I**, and **P**. They all hang or fall together. Let us look, then, at the points we have dealt with so far, and see how irresistible grace depends on them.

A. Limited atonement

The Bible teaches that from eternity God foreloved certain people, and that He therefore sent His Son to die for them. As we have seen, Jesus actually did die for them. He did not just pretend to take away their sins. He did not theoretically go to hell for them. He actually did bear their sins and take their guilt away. It is either-or. Either Jesus saved them or He did not. Either He was an actual substitute or He was not. The Bible teaches He was.

If Christ has actually made them free from the guilt of sin, and if salvation comes only by faith, then it is necessary for God to send His Holy Spirit into their lives in order that they may accept the salvation that has already been worked out for them on the cross. The Holy Spirit must work in an irresistible way. Acceptance of Christ cannot be left partially to man, for then all would refuse, and Christ's atonement would have been in vain. Thus limited atonement points to the irresistible work of the Holy Spirit.

B. Unconditional election

If it is true that God has unconditionally elected some to be saved (we will not repeat the innumerable Scripture evidences given in chap. 2), then, of course, the Spirit has to work in an irresistible way. Otherwise, everyone because of his depravity would reject Christ, and then there would be no foreordination to eternal life. God could not be sure that those whom He elected would believe and be saved. The certainty of election means that the Spirit works certainly and that He accomplishes what God foreordained. Without the irresistible grace of God, there could be no foreordination or election.

1. *John 6:37, 44*

"All that the Father gives me will come to me, and whoever comes to me I will never drive away. . . . No one can come to me, unless the Father who sent me draws him, and I will raise him up at the last day."

Jesus says here that the Father has given certain people to Jesus, and that every single one of them "will come to me." There is no indefiniteness. It is a simple declarative statement: "All . . . will come to me." That can occur, of course, only if God irresistibly causes them to come.

And that is what Jesus says will happen (v. 44). The Father *will* draw them and Jesus *will* then raise them up in the last day. That word "draw" is the same word that is used of drawing a net of fish (John 21:6, 11). Such a fishnet cannot resist Peter as he drags it ashore. It is helpless and passive; it cannot fight back. It is the same word that is used of Peter when he draws his sword to cut off the ear of Malchus (John 18:10), or of Paul and Silas being dragged into the market place (Acts 16:19), or of Paul being dragged by a mob out of the temple (Acts 21:30). In each of these cases, the object is drawn irresistibly. The sword cannot resist Peter, nor Paul the mob. Neither can those whom the Father has given to Jesus resist the Father as He draws them. Every single one that the omnipotent Father gives to Jesus will come to Jesus. It is as certain as Jesus' word is certain.

2. John 10:16

"I have the other sheep that are not of this flock. I must bring them also. They too will listen to my voice, and there will be one flock and one shepherd." Jesus infallibly secures all His sheep. Some belong to the flock already, others do not. Those that do not He will certainly bring into the fold. He does this by sending the Holy Spirit to work in their lives and to draw them irresistibly to the fold. Then there will be one flock and one shepherd.

3. Romans 8:29-30

"For whom he foreknew he also foreordained to become conformed to the image of his Son that he might be the first-born among many brethren; and whom he foreordained, these he also called; and whom he called, these he also justified; and whom he justified these he also glorified."

Let us first clarify a couple of terms. As we have seen before, the word "foreknew" means "foreloved." It means the same as in Genesis 4:1, which states that Adam knew Eve. The word "called" does not only refer to an external, verbal call; but in accord with the rest of the New Testament, it means in addition to the external call the working by God of an inward affirmative response.

Thus Paul clearly states that there is an inexorable course of events beginning with the eternal love of God for the elect. Those whom God has foreloved, He has foreordained. And whom He has foreordained He has also called so that they will believe. And those whom He has called, and who have believed, He has justified (declared righteous). And whom He has justified He has glorified. God is not frustrated in His plans. There is a finality and certainty ringing through the whole process from God's love and foreordination to final glorification. Well, such finality and certainty can come about only if God works irresistibly in the lives of those whom He has foreloved.

C. Total depravity

All the Biblical illustrations of the new birth, which presupposes man's total inability or depravity, indicate that man is unable to resist God's purposes in election.

1. *Resurrection*

The Bible claims that natural man is dead in his sins. He has no spiritual life. A dead man cannot resist the resurrecting powers of God. At the Day of Judgment everybody will be resurrected from the dead. Some will wish that they would not have to be. They will cry for the mountains to fall on them in order to annihilate them, for they are afraid to meet their God and Judge. But they cannot resist. God will resurrect everyone who has died — good and bad, believer and disbeliever. They can no more refuse to be resurrected than God can break His promise to resurrect everyone.

When Lazarus was in the grave and Christ gave him life, he could not remain dead: he had to come out of the grave. Christ could not be frustrated in His desire to give him life.

In the same way, when God resurrects someone from spiritual death, it is impossible for the dead one to resist. He has to be made alive. He cannot do anything about it.

2. *New birth*

A second illustration of God's work in man's heart is birth. Now it is obviously foolish to speak of anybody refusing to be born. People have no choice about being born. It is entirely out of their hands. A person that is not, cannot refuse to be conceived and born.

Likewise, it is ridiculous to speak of anyone resisting spiritual birth. "The wind blows wherever it pleases. . . . So it is with everyone born of the Spirit" (John 3:8).

3. *A new creation*

Another illustration of regeneration is creation (II Cor. 5:17; Gal. 6:5; Eph. 2:10). Nothing that ever was created refused to be created. At one time there was nothing but God. When He decided to create the universe, nothing could say to Him, "I do not want to be created," for there was not even anything to say that. It was just created. God is omnipotent: He did what He wanted.

Similarly, in spiritual creation no one is able to resist God's purposes. God spiritually re-creates whom He will. And none can resist.

4. Workmanship

Paul writes that we are "God's workmanship created in Christ Jesus for good works" (Eph. 2:10). Just as a doll or a telephone or a radio cannot resist being made, neither can we who are God's workmanship refuse to be made.

Thus every Biblical illustration about regeneration teaches the natural total depravity of man and his inability not only to do good, but also his inability to resist the work of the Holy Spirit. To put it positively, Paul speaks of "how very great is his power at work in us who believe" (Eph. 1:19). "This power in us," Hebrews goes on to say, "is the same as the mighty strength that he used when he raised Christ from the dead and seated him at his right hand in heaven." What a pile-up of ideas to emphasize the powerful working of God in man!

Thank God for His irresistible grace. Without it no one would be saved.

At times God sends adversity to people by giving them poverty, disgrace, cancer, or loneliness. When someone is in trouble, it is natural to turn to another for help; and it would be natural to think they would turn to God. But man is so depraved, he will never turn unless the Spirit of God changes his heart.

Sometimes, instead of the vinegar approach, God uses the sugar approach. He blesses people with so many of this world's goods, that you would think that anybody with a grain of gratitude would turn to God, from whom all blessings flow. Yet some people, who never have to worry about money and who are in the best of health, seem to become more indifferent and calloused to God the more blessings they receive. The reason? The Holy Spirit is not working in their lives.

It is even possible for a person to see miracles and yet not believe, if the Spirit is not in his life. This is what happened when the Pharisees saw the Son of God healing a blind man and yet called Him Beelzebub. If someone should even come back from the dead, they would not believe, said Abraham to the rich man (Luke 16). The reason is that the natural man is unable to accept the things of God unless the Spirit of God changes him.

Or a person can hear prophetic preaching about the Day of Judgment and yet laugh the preacher to scorn, as they did in the days of Noah. Or a preacher can be ever so eloquent, polished, emotional, and logical; but if the Spirit is not working, no one will believe.

So thank God for His irresistible grace. Without it, man is lost. If he has to give the least consent in order to be saved, he will be lost, so evil is he. He will resist. But thank God for His irresistible grace, whereby the total depravity of man is overcome, man is born again, and man believes.

This is what happened to Paul. He hated God so much he tried to throw in jail people who believed in Christ. Yet in spite of all his hate, and right in the midst of a hateful journey to Damascus, God came into his life in an irresistible way. Paul was overwhelmed. He could do nothing else but believe. That is irresistible grace.

Four centuries later an African, born of a Christian mother and a pagan father, tried to find peace. He first of all tried to live it up. He lived the most profligate life possible. He did just what he wanted to do, breaking God's commandments. He tried the pagan religion of Manicheanism. He tried logic and the university. All to no avail, until one day he was in a garden and he heard a voice say, "Take, read; take, read." He ran out of the garden to his friend Alypsius, picked up the Bible, opened it at random to Romans 13:13, 14 and read, "Not in carousing and drunkenness, not in sexual promiscuity and sensuality, not in strife and jealousy. But put on the Lord Jesus Christ and make no provision for the flesh in regard to its lusts." Peace came over Augustine's soul and he said to his friend, "I have been regenerated."

That is the way God works. In the midst of our selfishness and hardness of heart, He often comes to the most unlikely person and with an irresistible force regenerates him so that he turns about and has peace with God.

Often Christians testify that they did not turn to God. No, it was in spite of themselves. They could not help themselves. In some mysterious way they were powerfully drawn to God (John 6:37, 44).

On one occasion Paul had for some time been preaching in Philippi by a river. A Thyatiran lady, a seller of purple goods, listened to Paul but she did not believe. Then Luke tells us that God opened her heart so that she would respond to things spoken by Paul (Acts 16:14). Without that opening of the heart, Lydia could not have believed. That is irresistible grace, and for it we must be thankful. Without it, we would all still be dead in our sins, unregenerated, unsaved.

A final word of caution is necessary. Although it is true that none would be saved were it not for the irresistible grace of God, no one may ever fall into the rationalistic trap of saying that he has nothing to do. He may not reason that since all depends on the Holy Spirit, he does not need to believe; or that he must simply wait for the Spirit to move him, and there is nothing that he can do to be saved.

Without denying for a moment the truth of irresistible grace — and this whole chapter has been devoted to it — nevertheless it is true that the Bible does not want us to reason in an unbiblical fashion and say that we will wait until the Spirit moves us before we believe. The Bible never allows that. It comes with only one command: Believe on the Lord Jesus Christ. Now, if you do believe, then you can know from the rest of the Bible it was because of God working in you both to will and to do according to His good pleasure (Phil. 2:13). So believe. God commands you to. But if you do, thank God for causing you to do so.

DISCUSSION QUESTIONS

1. Read what the Canons of Dort say about irresistible grace (III–IV, 10-14).
2. What does the word *grace* mean in the term *irresistible grace?*
3. What does *irresistible* mean?
4. Could the word *irresistible* be misunderstood? How?
5. What other words could be used instead of *irresistible?*
6. What is the ultimate cause of a person's accepting Christ?
7. Does the answer to question 6 do away with human responsibility? Why not?
8. Explain the Arminian position on irresistible grace.
9. What does John 6:37, 44 say about irresistible grace?
10. What does John 10:16 say about irresistible grace?
11. Turn to Romans 8:29-30 and show how it teaches irresistible grace.
12. How do the illustrations of regeneration (new birth, resurrection, creation, and workmanship) show that man cannot resist the Holy Spirit?
13. How does unconditional election point to irresistible grace?

14. How does the story of Lydia show that the mere outward presentation of the gospel is not enough to save a person, but that the person must be regenerated first (Acts 16:14)?
15. Show how the Arminian often assumes the fact of irresistible grace in his prayers.
16. Why is the teaching of irresistible grace such a wonderful one? Be personal in your answer.
17. Can you cite any people that you personally know of who in spite of themselves felt compelled to turn to Jesus to be saved?
18. Describe one person about whom you are inclined to say, "The only hope is that God will work in him with His irresistible grace."
19. Does the teaching of election prevent you from praying that God will work irresistibly? Why?

5

perseverance
of the saints

I. ITS DEFINITION

A. Once saved, always saved

The simplest, shortest description of the perseverance of the saints is: Once saved, always saved. It is one of the grandest thoughts in the Bible: Once you believe, you can never be lost, you can never go to hell. Christ will always be your Savior. It is possible to get your eternal destiny settled once for all so that you never have to worry about it.

B. Perseverance of the saints

The term *perseverance of the saints* emphasizes that Christians — saints, as Paul calls them in his letters — will persevere in trusting in Christ as their Savior. They will not turn on and then turn off, but they will continue believing forever. Thus they will always be saved.

C. Perseverance of God

It is possible, however, to use another term to describe this fact, namely, the perseverance of God. For really the perseverance of the saints depends on the perseverance of God. It is because God perseveres in His love toward His church that the church perseveres in its love toward Him.

The perseverance of the saints could be compared to the providence of God. In the natural world God not only created the universe, but He also upholds it. If He should withdraw His power for a second, the universe would go crashing back into nonexistence. God creates and sustains the universe. The same is true of our spiritual life. God not only re-created us, but He keeps us alive spiritually every moment. If He should withdraw His Holy Spirit from us for a single moment, we, too, would instantly crash back to our natural, depraved natures.

Or to use another illustration, we may be compared to a man living in an oxygen tent. He is kept alive only by this means outside of himself. Take the tent away and the man will die.

So it is the continuing perseverance of God that is the basis for the perseverance of the saints.

D. Preservation of the saints

Another term that could be used is *preservation of the saints.* Whereas the term *perseverance of the saints* emphasizes the activity of the Christian, the term *preservation of the saints* emphasizes the activity of God. Perseverance of the saints stresses that man does something, and perseverance of God stresses that God does it. Preservation of the saints, however, teaches that man is preserved by God. He is kept and guarded so that no one will snatch him out of God's hand.

E. Eternal security

In other words, perseverance of the saints means eternal security. The person who sincerely puts his trust in Christ as his Savior is safe in the arms of Jesus. He is secure. No one can hurt him. He will go to heaven. And this is for eternity. He is secure for all time, not just for a little while. He is eternally secure.

Arminianism teaches the opposite; namely, that a man who is truly born again, who is saved by the death of Jesus, can lose his faith and thus go to hell. Arminianism believes: in again, out again; now saved, now lost; first a child of God, then a child of the devil; now spiritually alive, now dead. Who can tell what his final state will be?

II. ITS SCRIPTURAL BASIS

A. Unconditional election

All the Five Points of Calvinism hang or fall together. The doctrine of the perseverance of the saints naturally follows from the Biblical fact of unconditional election. If the doctrine of election is false, then this doctrine is false, too; but if the doctrine of election is true, then this doctrine necessarily follows.

Election means that God has chosen some from eternity to be saved. He has ordained with divine certainty that they will go to heaven. If it were possible, as the Arminian says, for a person whom God elected to slip away from the faith after he had already begun to believe, then there is no election. Election means that God has foreordained that the elect will be saved. They can never perish. Well, that is perseverance of the saints.

In Romans 8:29 Paul says that those whom God foreknew — that is, foreloved — He also foreordained to heaven, and those whom He foreordained He also called, justified, and glorified. If a person could fall away and go to hell, then there would be no foreordination. But Paul is convinced that nothing can separate the elect from Christ's electing love. Tribulation cannot, nor anguish, nor persecution, nor famine, nor nakedness, nor peril, nor the sword. No, in all these things the Christians are more than conquerors through God who loves them. Moreover, says Paul, there is nothing — nothing at all — that can separate any Christian from God's love. "For I am persuaded that neither death, nor life, nor angels, nor principalities, nor things present, nor things to come, nor powers, nor height, nor depth, nor any other creature will be able to separate us from God's love" (Rom. 8:38, 39). This is the perseverance of the saints. There is absolutely nothing in all this world — past, present, or future — that can separate a believer from God's love toward him.

Really the perseverance of the saints depends on the perseverance of God. If it were true that man's faith ultimately comes from himself and not from God, then, because man is depraved, it would be very possible that changeable man would not persevere in believing, but might reject Christ one day. He believed once, but maybe tomorrow he will be emotionally disturbed and will take it all back. Maybe he will get some hard knocks and will blame God for them. Being fickle, he may get out of the wrong side of the bed and turn against God. It is very understandable on the Arminian theory of man being the cooriginator of his faith, that man could lose his faith and fall away.

But when we realize that faith is not man's gift to God, but is rather God's gift to man, then we realize that man will never lose his faith. This is dependable because God is not fickle. "I, the Lord, change not" (Mal. 3:6). "Jesus Christ is the same yesterday and today, yea and forever" (Heb. 13:8). God is not like a little boy who likes his teddy bear today but tomorrow he throws it in the corner. He is not like a girl who raves over her hair-do today but tomorrow tries another kind. No, God is not capricious, fickle, or erratic. He knows the beginning from the end. He perseveres in His love. He is stable and unchanging. It is this fact that causes Paul to write the Philippians that he is "confident of this very thing, that he who began a good work in you will perfect until the day of Jesus Christ." If God begins a work, He will finish it. If He started a work in the Philippians, then He will carry it through to the second coming of Christ. That is nothing else than the perseverance of the saints. The perseverance of the saints depends on the perseverance of God.

Or if it is thought that God chooses us to be saved because we have done some good such as believing on Christ, then it would be conceivable that if God sees us waver in our faith, He might change His mind so that we would be lost. For we are evil and depraved, and will turn away from God unless He comes into our lives every moment with His renewing and sustaining grace.

But that is not the way God works. He did not give us saving grace because He foresaw that we were going to do good, such as believe on Christ. For we are by nature totally depraved. There is nothing within us that could be the minutest, most microscopic cause of His loving us. Rather, everything within us would cause Him to hate us (see chap. 1). The cause for His loving us is to be found in Him alone. If God knew from the very first that there was absolutely nothing in us that would make us worthy in the slightest degree of receiving His love and saving grace, then there could be nothing in us such as sin or unbelief that would cause Him to turn His love away from us and to remove His saving grace. For the cause of His love is to be found in Him and not in us. Thus the Biblical doctrine of the perseverance of the saints is founded on the eternal, electing love of God.

B. Limited atonement

If what we have written in chapter 3 is true and Biblical, if Christ died for the elect, for God's sheep, then the perseverance of the saints naturally follows. The crucial question is: What did Christ actually do on the cross? Did He actually take away the guilt of His people? Or did He just do it theoretically? If Jesus was actually damned by God for the sins of His people, as Paul says He was in Galatians 3:13, if Christ really bore hellish pain on the cross and was a real — not just a paper — substitute for all the sins of His people, past, present, and future, then those people cannot go to hell and be punished for their sins. Christ was punished for them. This means that they will surely go to heaven. That is the perseverance of the saints.

In Romans 8:33-34 Paul reasons that way. He says that Christ was delivered up for us all, that is, the elect. That's limited atonement. Therefore, asks Paul, "Who will bring any charge against God's elect? God is the one who justifies. Who is the one who condemns? It is Christ who died" (Rom. 8:33, 34). Thus the atonement of Christ is another basis for the Christian's confidence that all those for whom Christ died will surely be saved. That is nothing else than the perseverance of the saints.

We say it is another basis. It really is not. For Christ's atonement for His people stems directly from the Father's electing love for His people. The atonement is merely implementing the electing love of the Father. The Father wanted to save them, and Christ does save them. In other words, there is unity between the objects of the Father's special love and the objects of Christ's atonement.

C. Eternal life

One of the most potent Biblical arguments for eternal security is found in the words *eternal life,* or *everlasting life.* The Bible constantly uses this term. Here are just four examples in John:

> "For God so loved the world that he gave his only Son, that whoever believes in him shall not perish but have everlasting life" (John 3:16).

> "He that believes on the Son has eternal life" (John 3:36).

> "Whoever hears my word and believes him who sent me has eternal life and will not be condemned" (John 5:24).

> "These things I have written to you who believe on the name of the Son of God that you may know that you have eternal life" (I John 5:13).

Both Jesus and John say that the believer has eternal life. First of all, note the tense of the verb. The believer *has* eternal life. Not that he will get it in the future, but that he has it right now. Anybody reading these lines may have, right now, without waiting a moment, eternal life. Jesus said so. All he has to do is to sincerely ask Jesus to be his Savior.

Then observe that it is *eternal* life. That means the life is forever. Or once saved, always saved: always, forever. If the

Arminian theory was true, and a born-again believer could lose his faith and become lost, then the last thing he could say is that the believer has eternal life. He could say that he has a good life, or a holy life, or a supernatural life, or a happy life; but he could never say that he has eternal life. For according to the Arminian he does not have eternal life. He has temporal life, life for a time being, a finite life, but not life that goes on without end.

Now this is contrary to the Word of God. Jesus says that "whosoever believes on the Son shall never perish." But the Arminian says, "Wait and see. Maybe he will go to hell." Jesus says, "He has eternal life." But the Arminian says, "No, for some it is only temporal life." Jesus says, "If a man eats of this bread, he will live forever" (John 6:51). The Arminian says, "Maybe." Jesus says, "I am the resurrection and the life. He who believes in me, even though he dies, yet will he live; and whoever lives and believes on me will never die" (John 11:25). "Never," says Jesus. "Possibly," says the Arminian.

Despite the Arminian, the constant use of the word *eternal* should bring joy to anybody who really believes. For the unequivocal testimony of the Bible is that he that trusts on Jesus will never die but will have a life that never, never ends. Thank God for eternal life.

D. John 6:39

"And this is the will of him who sent me, that I shall lose none of all that he has given me, but raise it up the last day."

Jesus has just said that all those whom the Father has given to Him will come to Him (v. 37). It is certain. Moreover, He has come to do the Father's will, and this is His will: to "lose none of all that he has given me" and to "raise them up at the last day." And in verse 44 He says that He "will raise him up at the last day." The "last day" refers to the last day on earth, the Day of Judgment. In other words, all who go to Jesus will be raised in the last day to go to heaven. Jesus will not lose one of them. This is the perseverance of the saints.

E. John 10:28-29

Speaking of His sheep, Jesus says, "I give them eternal life, and they will never perish; no one can snatch them out of my hand. My Father, who has given them to me, is greater than all; no one can snatch them out of my Father's hand."

If ever there was a single passage that clearly teaches eternal security, this is it. See the piling up of the arguments by Jesus:

1. *"Eternal life"*

This term alone is sufficient to prove the perseverance of the saints. For if a person departs from the faith once he has believed, then there is nothing eternal about the life Jesus promises him. There is a brief life, a short one, but not an eternal one. But Jesus says that it is an eternal life.

2. *"And they will never perish"*

If, as the Arminian says, a believer can lose his faith, then he will indeed perish. But Jesus says he will never perish. The evidence for the perseverance of the saints could hardly be clearer; but just in case there are still some doubting Thomases, Jesus adds a third statement that cuts off any remaining fears.

3. *"No one can snatch them out of my hand"*

How definite Jesus is! No one can cause a single one to be lost. The devil cannot do it. Teachers cannot. Friends cannot. Even you cannot snatch yourself out of Jesus' hands. It is impossible. No one can do it.

Certainly now there should be no more questionings in the minds of any concerning Jesus' teaching about eternal security. These three unequivocal statements are conclusive. But just to make absolutely sure that there is no misunderstanding, Jesus adds a fourth statement.

4. *"My Father, who has given them to me, is greater than all; no one can snatch them out of my Father's hand"*

The Father is omnipotent. He is bigger and stronger than all people and devils put together. Therefore, the inescapable conclusion is that no one can snatch the sheep of God out of His hand. What a powerful conclusion and restatement of the preservation of the saints! If anybody does not believe now in eternal security, then he is blind.

F. Ephesians 1:13, 14

"Having also believed, you were sealed in him with the Holy Spirit of promise, who is given as a pledge of our inheritance."

In the New Testament days, letters or objects, such as Jesus' grave (Matt. 27:66), were sealed. The seal was used to guarantee the genuineness of the article, to indicate that it belonged to someone, and to protect it. Thus the possession of the Holy Spirit was God's seal — an indication that the believer belonged to God and that he would be guarded against harm. In Ephesians 1:13-14 and 4:30 Paul says that that sealing or guarding will be effective right down to the day of redemption. The Holy Spirit is a guarantee that they will not be lost.

Then Paul uses another striking illustration to teach eternal security. He says that the Holy Spirit is a down payment ("pledge" in the King James Version) of the complete inheritance that is yet to come (Eph. 1:14). The Greek word for "pledge" or "down payment" is the ordinary word that was used in business transactions or other agreements. A first installment was made, just as in today's credit world; and that payment was a pledge that the rest would follow. So the Holy Spirit is God's pledge that the full inheritance will follow. That is the same as saying that once you have the Holy Spirit, you will always have the Holy Spirit and more, too. Or, once saved, always saved.

G. I Peter 1:4, 5

"to obtain an inheritance . . . reserved in heaven for you, who are guarded by the power of God through faith for a salvation ready to be revealed in the last time."

Peter is very comforting about the eternal certainty of our salvation. He says that the Christian has an inheritance and that it is kept in heaven for him. But maybe, someone worries, the inheritance is there, but he will never get there. He thinks he is too weak a Christian.

To fend off such an idea, Peter says that the Christian is guarded for this salvation. The word "guarded" is the same one that is used of protecting and guarding a city by soldiers (II Cor. 11:32). But Peter emphasizes that the Christian is not guarded by such weak human elements as soldiers. No, he is protected by God Himself. And God is omnipotent. As if it were not enough to simply say "God," Peter drives home his point of the might of God by adding the word "power." The Christian is kept by "the power of God."

It might be possible for someone to agree that Peter meant that the Christian is guarded by the power of God, but that it was only for a short time. Peter squelches that idea quickly by adding that God keeps him for the salvation that is to be revealed in the last time, in the Day of Judgment. The preservation of the saints is not for a day, but it is forever, right down to the last day of time.

III. SOME TRADITIONAL OBJECTIONS

A. Do we not all know people who at one time expressed a faith in Christ? They went to church, read God's Word, prayed, and seemed to be genuine Christians. Then something happened and gradually they departed from the faith until today they will have nothing to do with the church, Christ, or God. Do not these actual case histories prove that the perseverance of the saints is not true?

In response to this objection, let us divide the answer into two parts:

1. Christians

It is true that Christians can backslide. We have all had that experience to some degree. At times we do not seem to be as close to God as we should. We become spiritually cold to a greater or lesser degree. And some Christians do some pretty bad things. You would hardly know they were Christians. There are adulteries and murders by Davids, denials of Christ by Peters, and the doing of things that ought not to be done by Pauls.

But the doctrine of the perseverance of the saints does not mean that Christians are sinless. The Bible teaches us that the Christian will sin and in some cases he will backslide a great deal. But if he is truly born again, if the Holy Spirit was really in him, causing him to believe, then the Spirit is a down payment of his full inheritance. Then he really does have eternal life, which means that he will be eternally saved.

The Bible does not promise that the Christian life will always be in a straight line upward. Rather it may be like a small boy climbing a snowy hill. He frequently slips, but he does manage to get to the top.

The Christian life is like a chart line of the American economy over a period of a hundred years. It begins in the lower left corner and rises to the upper right hand corner. There are ups and downs, there are recessions and near catastrophic depressions. The line is jagged and not straight in its upward climb;

but when viewed over a period of a hundred years, it is easy to see that in spite of temporary setbacks there is ultimately a gain, and that our economy is far superior to that of the nineteenth century.

Or, as the great Calvinistic Baptist, Charles Spurgeon, put it, a man on board ship may be knocked down on the deck by the waves again and again, but he is never washed overboard.

Paul affirms this fact of the ups and downs of the Christian life and yet of the perseverance of the saints, when, in that same section in Romans where he writes about the grievous sins that come into a Christian's life, he says that nevertheless, in spite of all these setbacks, "sin will not have dominion over you" (6:14). In other words, the Christian may suffer temporary defeats, but sin will never gain complete control in him. There will always be a fighting against sin even though he is weak. This is true just because God has not taken His Holy Spirit from the Christian. Thus the fact that a Christian is still warring against sin and even falls does not mean that he will one day be abandoned by God to complete domination by sin. Paul says it plainly: "Sin will not have dominion over you."

So, one answer to this problem of apparent defections from the Christian faith is that some of the backslidings that we see may be only temporary setbacks of a stumbling Christian, who, by the grace of the Holy Spirit, will eventually come back fully to the faith he seems to have denied.

2. Non-Christians

Another explanation is that the denying persons may not have been Christians after all. Not everybody who says, "Lord, Lord," is a Christian. Some have a form of godliness but deny its power (II Tim. 3:5). Some, like Judas, can even preach the gospel and perform miracles and yet be lost. Others will appear as angels of light, but in reality they are devils (II Cor. 11:14). Some people will say, "Lord, Lord, did we not prophesy in your name, and in your name cast out demons, and in your name do mighty works?" But Jesus will say to them, "Depart from me, you who work evil" (Matt. 7:22-23). Some seed will fall on shallow soil. It will take root quickly and spring up, but the sun will soon scorch it and it will die. So some people will hear an evangelistic message, be emotionally aroused, go forward joyfully in response to the altar call, and then in two months forget that they ever responded to Christ.

Instead of such cases proving that the Christian can fall away from the faith, these many examples warn us that we must make our calling and election sure (II Peter 1:10). They point out the fact that it is possible to have an external faith and yet not to be a Christian. It is possible to belong to a church, to be baptized, and to partake of the Lord's Supper, and yet go to hell. "They are not all Israel who are desended from Israel" (Rom. 9:6). Not everybody in the church belongs to the true church. We must be sure that we are born again, that we are sorry for our sins, and that we sincerely ask Christ to be our Savior.

Thus these actual historical examples of people backsliding do not militate against the Biblical teaching of the preservation of the saints. For these people are either Christians who are temporarily backsliding, but who will be restored fully to the faith, or they are pretenders, who never were real, born-again Christians. For the Biblical evidence is too overwhelmingly on the side of "once saved, always saved."

B. Will not a belief in the perseverance of the saints cause some to become licentious? Will they not reason that if they are eternally secure and can never be lost, then they can do anything they want? They can live it up and sin, for they will always be saved?

I have news for anybody who thinks in that way: Such a person is not demonstrating that he is a Christian; and if he perseveres in that kind of thinking, he will go to hell instead of to heaven. For it is impossible for a born-again Christian to take such an attitude. The Holy Spirit will not let him. If God has begun a good work in someone, He will not then abandon him to all kinds of sin. "Sin will not have dominion over him" (Rom. 6:14). It is simply a contradiction in terms to speak of a Christian who can do anything that his old sinful self desires. When God predestines someone, He predestines him to holiness, not licentiousness (Eph. 1:4). If anyone says that it does not matter what he does because God has predestined him, then he cannot say that he has been predestined; for predestined people never act in such a sinful way.

When we say, "Once saved, always saved," that does not mean only being saved from the guilt of sin, so that the saved will escape the wrath of hell. It means also to be saved from the power of sin. Salvation is never simply salvation from the guilt of sin but not from the power of sin. It is both. It is impossible for anyone to be saved from the guilt of sin without being saved from the power of sin.

Perseverance of the saints means that the saints will persevere in their faith. And that faith is composed of sorrow and repentance from sin. If anyone is not sorry for his sins and abandons himself to them, then he never had faith in the first place and he is not saved.

The term *preservation of the saints* means that God will preserve, protect, and guard them unto a salvation ready to be revealed in the last time. That salvation does not mean simply that they are saved from hell but can now sin all they want. Such a situation would be hell in heaven, and that is impossible.

Furthermore, it is exactly when a Christian fully realizes the Biblical truth of the perseverance of the saints, that he will not be inclined to licentiousness but to holiness. For he will want to thank God for keeping him in the faith, and the best way he can do that is by keeping God's commandments. When a Christian realizes that he is not innately a good person, but rather by nature is a hater of God; when he realizes further that the faith he does have came to him from God; and when he realizes that the only reason he perseveres in believing in God is that God is persevering in sending the Spirit into his life — then he does not want to sin, but wants to thank God for never stopping that good work that He began in him (Phil. 1:6).

So it is a complete caricature of the Christian faith to assert that the doctrine of the perseverance of the saints leads to licentiousness. The exact opposite is true.

Conclusion

The teaching of "once saved, always saved" is one of the grandest of Biblical teachings. Let no one rob you of the joy of knowing that you will be saved forever. What a blessing it is to be able to make a decision once and for all about your eternal destiny. How good it is to be able to commit your life to Christ, and to know that as soon as you do you will always be saved and will be guarded by the power of God unto the full salvation to be revealed when Christ returns.

Praise God from whom all blessings flow. Praise the Father for His electing love. Praise the Son for His atoning death. Praise the Holy Spirit for His irresistible work. Praise the Triune God for preserving us to the end. Praise God!

DISCUSSION QUESTIONS

1. Read the Canons of Dort (V). Discuss the first thought you come across that is new for you.
2. Discuss the meaning of the following terms:
   a. eternal security
   b. preservation of the saints
   c. perseverance of God
   d. perseverance of the saints
3. How are the four previous terms related to each other?
4. Turn to Romans 8:29, 30, 38, and 39; show how unconditional election necessarily leads to the perseverance of the saints.
5. Why must the perseverance of the saints necessarily be so if the atonement of Christ is limited to the elect and is substitutionary?
6. How do the many Bible texts that speak of eternal or everlasting life prove this doctrine?
7. Turn to John 10:28-29 and show four ways in which this text asserts that "once saved, always saved."
8. Does backsliding disprove the perseverance of the saints? Why?
9. Does the fact that some apparent Christians — such as Judas, Hymeneus, and Alexander — eventually rejected the gospel, militate against the perseverance of the saints? Why?
10. Why can you learn from their examples?
11. How do you reconcile the preservation of the saints with the unpardonable sin mentioned in Hebrews 6:4-6 and Matthew 12:31?
12. How would you answer a person who said, "If the perseverance of the saints is true, then why not go out and sin all you want, since you will be saved in the end anyhow?"
13. Somebody says to you, "I wish I could be sure I will always be saved." How do you help him?
14. How can the knowledge of the fact of the perseverance of the saints be a great joy for you?
15. Do you know of anyone who seemed to be a Christian but now denies Christ either by words or actions or both? Tell about it. How do you explain it? Could it happen to you? Why?
16. How can you be assured of your eternal salvation?

6

the great mystery

I. THE PROBLEM

For five chapters, the sovereignty of God has been emphasized.

The Biblical doctrine of *total depravity* emphasizes that natural, unregenerated man is never able to do a single good thing for even a fraction of a second. He is dead to good actions. If he is ever to believe, or to do anything that is good, it will come about only when God causes him to do so.

Unconditional election teaches God's sovereignty by pointing out that God's selection of man for life eternal is not based on anything in man. His choice is not conditioned by His foreknowing who would cooperate with Him and accept the sacrifice of Christ. It is an unconditional election. The reason for the sovereign choice is found in God alone and not in anything man is or does.

We see God's sovereignty in *limited atonement* when we realize that Christ did not make an atonement that saves all the world, but rather one which saves only those who have been chosen by the Father. There is complete unity between the purpose of the Father and the Son. The Son died for those whom the Father loved.

When we observe the selectivity of *irresistible grace,* we again see the sovereignty of God. Just as nothingness cannot refuse to be created or born, just as the dead cannot resist being made alive, so the spiritually dead and unborn cannot resist the omnipotent Spirit of God in being born again. And if anyone does have spiritual life, it is because the Spirit is carrying out the sovereign choice of the Father. Man can do nothing about being born again.

There is a unity among the three Persons of the Trinity. The Father chooses the elect, Christ dies for them, and the Holy

Spirit carries out the will of both by irresistibly causing the elect to believe and be saved.

The *perseverance of the saints* reveals the sovereignty of God in that it is a continuation of His sovereignty as seen in the T, U, L, and I of TULIP.

To emphasize the sovereignty of God even more, it is necessary to point out that everything is foreordained by God. Not only is God omnipotent, so that to Him the nations are a drop in the bucket or as a fine coating of dust on weighing scales (Isa. 40), but He also "works all things according to the counsel of his will" (Eph. 1:11).

It is even Biblical to say that God has foreordained sin. If sin was outside the plan of God, then not a single important affair of life would be ruled by God. For what action of man is perfectly good? All of history would then be outside of God's foreordination: the fall of Adam, the crucifixion of Christ, the conquests of the Roman Empire, the battle of Hastings, the Reformation, the French Revolution, Waterloo, the American Revolution, the Civil War, two World Wars, presidential assassinations, racial violence, and the rise and fall of nations.

In two instances the Bible is especially clear in teaching that everything, including sin, is ordained by God: the selling of Joseph and the crucifixion of Christ.

In the first, note the sin involved. Joseph's brothers hated him. They carefully premeditated how to get rid of him, threw him in a well, and later sold him in slavery to some complete strangers who were headed for Egypt. Then they went home with Joseph's coat smeared with the blood of an animal and cruelly lied to their father, who had a special love for Joseph. There can be no question of the fact that they sinned.

But now notice what Joseph says about them when later they go to Egypt to buy some food. He says: "You did not do it" (Gen. 45:8). In a sense, this is incorrect. His brothers did do it. They deliberately, maliciously, hatefully sold Joseph into slavery. But Joseph says they did not. Joseph is not wrong, but is only trying to say in a forceful, striking way that God was really back of it all. The sinful act of selling was not left to chance or man's sinful will. God was determined that Joseph would go to Egypt. So he says, "You did not do it," and then immediately makes a statement that most people would never dare to make: "but God did." God made sure that Joseph would be sold into Egypt.

Later Joseph acknowledges more explicitly that his brothers

committed a sin, when he tells them, "You meant evil against me." But, he adds, "God meant it for good" (Gen. 50:20). The use of the same verb for both Joseph and God heightens the paradox. God is involved in a real way in the brothers' actions. God wanted to be sure that His chosen people in Israel had a special friend in Egypt who could help them in time of drought and starvation. For out of this people was to come the Savior of the world. In order, then, to accomplish His goal of continuing the line of Abraham, God could not leave it to chance. So He ordained the sin of Joseph's brothers: "God did it"; "God meant it for good." In other words, God made it absolutely certain that Joseph's brothers would sin; yet He did it in such a way that the brothers and not God are to blame. For God is only holiness and light, and there is no darkness in Him at all.

A second clear example of the foreordination of sin is the crucifixion of Christ. This was the most heinous sin of all because it was the epitome of man's hatred against God.

Yet this sin was ordained by God. God did not leave the death of His Son — and thus the salvation of His people — up to sinful man. Suppose Judas and the Jewish leaders had had a change of heart and decided not to kill Jesus. Suppose Jesus had grown old and had died a natural death or had never died. Then there would be no atonement for sin and no heaven. Then God's plans of election and salvation would have been thwarted.

God did not leave to chance the salvation of the world. So, as Peter said at Pentecost, Jesus was "delivered up by the determinate counsel and foreknowledge of God" (Acts 2:23). And later the church, speaking of the killing of Jesus, confessed to God that Herod, Pilate, the Gentiles, and the Jews had been "gathered together to do whatsoever your hand and counsel foreordained to come to pass" (Acts 4:28). In other words, sin is ordained by God.[1]

Thus, once again, we confess with full force the absolute sovereignty of God. He predestines, elects, and foreordains.

But, if anyone has really been thinking, he has probably raised a serious objection many times. Involuntarily, the average person rebels and almost recoils at some of these ideas. He boggles at the thought of everything having been planned and determined

---

[1]Compare Joshua 11:20; I Samuel 16:23; II Samuel 12:11-12; 16:10-11; I Kings 22:20-33; Job 1:21; Isaiah 10:5; II Thessalonians 2:11; and Revelation 17:17. Read in Article XIII of the Belgic Confession of Faith the magnificent statement concerning God's foreordination. (See pp. 98-100.)

by God so long ago. It bothers him. For, where is God's holiness? If he ordained the sin of Joseph's brothers and the sin of Judas, how can any rational person say that God is holy? Isn't God to blame?

Or, to say it in another way, where is man's freedom? Is man just a puppet that God is manipulating? Just a mechanical toy man with a big wind-up handle in his back to make him go? Is he just a computerized machine that is fed some data and then mechanically does its duty?

Where is man's responsibility if God has foreordained everything? Was not the author of *The Predestinated Thief* correct in polemicizing that a predestinated thief is not responsible for stealing? God is to blame.

Here is the great mystery, the title of this chapter: How to solve this overwhelming problem of reconciling God's foreordination and man's freedom. It is the mystery of divine sovereignty and human responsibility, of God's freedom and man's freedom, of God's love and God's omnipotence. How to reconcile the two?

II. SOLUTIONS

A. Arminianism

There are two ways to solve the problem: one is rationalistic and the other is Biblical. In spite of all the Arminian's appeal to the Bible, it is remarkable that at the point of God's sovereignty he appeals to reason instead of the Bible. He correctly sees the problem: reconciling the two opposing forces of God's sovereignty and man's responsibility.

But in solving the problem he substitutes man's reason for the Bible. He reasons that he cannot logically reconcile these two apparently contradictory facts. So he holds to one set of facts and denies the other. He holds to man's freedom and restricts God's sovereignty. In this way, he has no rational problem. The contradiction dissolves.

B. Hyper-Calvinism

Diametrically opposite to the Arminian is the hyper-Calvinist. He looks at both sets of facts — the sovereignty of God and the freedom of man — and, like the Arminian, says he cannot reconcile the two apparently contradictory forces. Like the Arminian, he solves the problem in a rationalistic way by denying one side of the problem. Whereas the Arminian denies the sovereignty of God, the hyper-Calvinist denies the responsibility of man. He sees the clear Biblical statements concerning God's foreordination and holds firmly to that. But being logically unable to reconcile it with man's responsibility, he denies the latter. Thus the Arminian and hyper-Calvinist, although poles apart, are really very close together in their rationalism.

C. Calvinism

1. A paradox

Over against these humanistic views, the Calvinist accepts both sides of the antinomy. He realizes that what he advocates is ridiculous. It is simply impossible for man to harmonize these two sets of data. To say on the one hand that God has made certain all that ever happens, and yet to say that man is responsible for what he does? Nonsense! It must be one or the other, but not both. To say that God foreordains the sin of Judas, and yet Judas is to blame? Foolishness! Logically the author of *The Predestinated Thief* was right. God cannot foreordain the theft and then blame the thief.

And the Calvinist freely admits that his position is illogical, ridiculous, nonsensical, and foolish. This is in accord with Paul, who said, "The word of the cross is to them that perish foolishness" (I Cor. 1:18). The Greeks seek after wisdom and logic, and to them the Calvinist is irrational. The Calvinist holds to two apparently contradictory positions.[2] He says on the one hand, God has foreordained all things. Then he turns around and says to every man, "Your salvation is up to you. You must believe. It is your duty and responsibility. And if you don't, you cannot blame God. You must blame only yourself. But if you do believe, remember that it was God who worked in you both to believe and to do according to His good pleasure" (Phil. 2:12, 13). "If you do press on to lay hold on the goal of life, remember that Christ laid hold on you that you might lay hold on it" (Phil. 3: 12). In the face of all logic, the Calvinist says that if man does anything good, God gets all the glory; and if man does anything bad, man gets all the blame. Man can't win.

To many people such a position seems foolish. It is unrea-

---

[2]It should be emphasized that the contradiction is only apparent and not real. Man cannot harmonize the two apparently contradictory positions, but God can.

sonable. So the Calvinist has to make up his mind: what is his authority? His own human reason or the Word of God?

If he answers, the human reasoning powers, then, like the Arminian and hyper-Calvinist, he will have to exclude one of the two parallel forces. But he cannot do that, for he believes the Bible is God's Word and that it was inspired by the Holy Spirit. He trusts God entirely, knowing that His Word cannot be broken. It is infallible and inerrant.

With that firm belief and a willingness to believe everything in it, he accepts this paradox of divine sovereignty and human responsibility. He cannot reconcile the two; but seeing that the Bible clearly teaches both, he accepts both.

2. A mystery

And it does not embarrass him that he cannot understand everything about God. After all, God's ways are higher than his ways, as the heavens are higher than the earth (Isa. 55:9). If he could understand everything, such as the problem of evil, then he would have a mind as great as God's. He remembers God's questions to Job, when Job could not understand all his troubles and doubted God's goodness. God asked Job: "Where were you when I laid the foundations of the earth? Tell me, if you have understanding." And then He adds sarcastically, "Surely, you know!" God goes on to show Job's smallness when He asks, "Have you commanded the morning, since your days began, and caused the dawn to know its place? Have you entered the springs of the sea? Have the gates of death been revealed to you? Declare if you know all this. . . . Where is the way to the dwelling of light, and where is the darkness?" "You know," God adds sarcastically, "for you were born then, and the number of your days is great!" (Job 38).

The point of God's questioning is to show Job that he is puny and that God is infinitely greater. Therefore, it is not surprising that Job does not have all the answers. After all, there are some things that God knows and man can never fathom, because God is infinitely and qualitatively greater than man.

The Calvinist's motto is Deuteronomy 29:29, where Moses says that "the secret things belong to the Lord our God; but the things that are revealed belong to us and to our children forever, that we may do all the words of the law." There are certain matters that are too deep for man. He cannot and never will compre-

hend them. He is finite and God is infinite. One of these matters is the apparent paradox of the sovereignty of God and the
responsibility of man. This secret matter belongs to the Lord our
God, and we should leave it there. We ought not to probe into
that secret counsel of God.

But there is plenty of God's will that has been revealed to us,
such as the command to believe, the moral law, the Ten Commandments, the Sermon on the Mount, and the method of becoming holy. There is no question about these matters, and man
should learn them, teach them to his children, and obey them.

This, then, is the religious humility of the Calvinist. He confesses: I don't know.[3] I can't understand everything; but since
it is in the Bible that God is one hundred percent sovereign and
yet that I am responsible, I believe. And all those things that
are commanded, I'll try to do them.

3. *The application*

This means that although man is totally depraved and unable to
believe, and that although faith is a gift of God produced by the
irresistible work of the Holy Spirit, nevertheless, it is up to man
to believe. He has the duty to obey God's command to believe.

It means that although sanctification is a gift of God, and
although it is God who works in us to do good things, nevertheless it is our responsibility to use the means of grace, and not
wait for God to move us.

It means that although God has foreordained everything, yet
prayer is efficacious, and man should pray, knowing that the
fervent prayer of a righteous man is powerful (James 5:16).

It means that although God has not elected all, or that although Christ has not died for all, nevertheless, we must be
zealous in following Christ's command to go into all the world,
making disciples of all nations (Matt. 28:19).

For this is the Biblical pattern, combining the two elements:

---

[3]The Christian must never be ashamed of saying, "I don't know." In
fact, learned ignorance is wiser than the wisdom of scoffers. Calvin wrote:
"Of those things which it is neither given nor lawful to know, ignorance is
learned; the craving to know, a kind of madness" (*Institutes of the Christian
Religion*, III, xxiii, 8). "Those who seek to know more than God has
revealed are *madmen!* Wherefore, let us delight ourselves more in wise
ignorance than in an immoderate and intoxicated curiosity to know more
than God permits" ("*The Eternal Predestination of God*," in *Calvin's
Calvinism*, p. 127).

the sovereignty of God and the responsibility of man. It is remarkable how Paul ties them together.

For example, before and after his great passage on divine election (Rom. 9–11), Paul presupposes human responsibility. Chapters 6 and 7 are replete with commands, such as, "Let not sin reign in your mortal bodies" and "Do not yield your members to sin."

And in the very next verse following the election passage, he starts out with, "I urge you, therefore, brothers, by the mercies of God that you present your bodies to God as a living sacrifice. And do not be conformed to this world, but be transformed" (Rom. 12:1). Notice that the basis for the strong appeal to action — the "therefore" — is found in the immediately preceding subject, namely, God's choice of Israel. For Paul, election does not kill initiative, but is the foundation for it.

Observe the same combination of God's sovereignty and man's responsibility in Colossians 3:12. Paul encourages the Colossians to put on a heart of compassion, kindness, humility, gentleness, and peace. His reason is that they have been elected by God. His thought is that since they have been chosen to be good and holy, they should live up to what is expected of them.

In I Thessalonians 5:8-9 he reasons in the same way. He urges the Thessalonians to be self-controlled, "because God has not destined us for wrath, but to obtain salvation."

And in II Thessalonians 2:15 he exhorts his readers to stand firm just because God has chosen them from the beginning to be saved (2:13-14).

In other words, for Paul, election, instead of killing initiative, was a stimulus to good actions.

III. THE PRACTICE

It is good to have theory, but it is also profitable to observe the practice. Does Calvinism extinguish the incentive to good deeds? If a person knows he has been elected, will not his desire to work hard for God be quenched? The answer can be seen in the lives of two who believed in the sovereignty of God with all their being: John Calvin and Paul.

A. Calvin

The energy and zeal of Calvin are unbelievable. Here is a man who believed so much in the sovereignty of God that later generations have almost identified his name with predestination. Yet look at his life, his energy, and zeal for work.

Stickelberger writes of his story in Geneva: "He was a relentless preacher of the Word. In addition to the Sunday worship service, every second week he held the daily weekday services. More than two thousand of these sermons are preserved. . . . Besides his preaching he delivered three lectures on theology during the week. He visited the sick and lackadaisical members. On Thursdays he conducted the Council of the elders, and on Fridays the preachers' meeting in which Holy Scripture was discussed. There was not a day when strangers did not visit him to receive his encouragement. The nights were devoted more to writing than to sleep."[4]

A hostile Catholic biographer writes: "It is almost unbelievable how a man who had to fight continually against serious bodily infirmities was able to unfold such a many-sided and fatiguing activity. Contemporaries have well compared him with a bow that is always strung. He robbed himself of sleep in order to devote his time to work and wearied even his secretaries with constant dictation. His home was always open to anyone seeking advice. At all times he was informed about all affairs of Church and state, even down to the most insignificant details. Although he had little contact with the outside world, he knew almost every single citizen."[5]

This gigantic work is all the more overwhelming when one considers that Calvin had so much sickness. Stickelberger writes: "As a consequence of his privations and vigils during his youth, early in his life he was afflicted with a headache concentrated on one side which hardly ever left him during his life. These pains were wont to enhance his emotional excitement to such an extent that during many a night he was 'inhumanly' tormented by them.

"Subjected to maladies of the trachea, he had with pains in his side to spit blood when he had used his voice too much in the pulpit. Several attacks of pleurisy prepared the way for consumption whose helpless victim he became at the age of fifty-one. Constantly he suffered from the hemorrhoidal vein, the pains of which were unbearably increased by an internal abscess that would not heal. Several times intermittent fever laid him low,

---

[4]Emanuel Stickelberger, *Calvin: A Life,* pp. 95-96.
[5]F. W. Kampschulte, *Johann Calvin* (Leipzig, 1899), II, 381, 382.

sapping his strength and constantly reducing it. He was plagued by gallstones and kidney stones in addition to stomach cramps and wicked intestinal influenzas. To all this there was finally added arthritis. It was no exaggeration when he parenthetically wrote in a letter, 'If only my condition were not a constant death struggle. . . .' "[6]

Remember that this energy and work were produced by the man whose name more than anyone else's in all history is associated with predestination. His life is a contradiction of the assertion that predestination kills a man's incentive to work. It would be difficult to name another who worked so indefatigably as the predestinationist John Calvin.

This seeming contradiction of predestination and humble trust in Jesus Christ is summed up beautifully in Calvin's will, which he dictated shortly before he died:

"In the name of God, I, John Calvin, servant of the Word of God in the Church of Geneva, weakened by many illnesses . . . thank God that He has shown not only mercy toward me, His poor creature, and . . . has suffered me in all sins and weaknesses but what is much more that He has made me a partaker of His grace to serve Him through my work. . . . I confess to live and die in this faith which He has given me, inasmuch as I have no other hope or refuge than His predestination upon which my entire salvation is grounded. I embrace the grace which He has offered me in our Lord Jesus Christ and accept the merits of His suffering and dying that through them all my sins are buried; and I humbly beg Him to wash me and cleanse me with the blood of our great Redeemer, as it was shed for all poor sinners so that I, when I shall appear before His face, may bear His likeness.

"Moreover, I declare that I endeavored to teach His Word undefiled and to expound Holy Scripture faithfully according to the measure of grace which He has given me. In all the disputations which I led against the enemies of the truth, I employed no cunning or any sophistry, but have fought his cause honestly. But, oh, my will, my zeal were so cold and sluggish that I know myself guilty in every respect; without His infinite goodness, all my passionate striving would only be smoke, indeed the grace itself which He gave me would make me even more guilty; thus my only confidence is that He is the Father

---

[6]Stickelberger, p. 86.

of mercy who as such desires to reveal Himself to such a miserable sinner.

"As for the rest, I desire that after my passing my body be buried according to the customary form in expectancy of the day of the blessed resurrection."[7]

O God, grant that we all may have such a simple trust in our only Savior Jesus Christ!

B. Paul

But do not stop with this giant in church history. Go back to the one who was the source for Calvin's thinking, the inspired apostle Paul. He was the one who said that those whom God foreloves He predestinates, and whom He predestinates He calls, and whom He calls He justifies and glorifies. It was Paul who said, "It is not of him that wills nor of him that runs, but of God that has mercy," and who quotes God as saying: "Jacob I loved and Esau I hated." "He will have mercy on whom he will have mercy, and whom he will he hardens." "Nay, but, O man, who are you to reply against God? Shall the thing formed say to him who formed it, why have you made me thus? Doesn't the potter have power over the clay?" It was Paul who spoke of those who had been chosen in Christ from before the foundation of the world to be holy and without blame, having predestinated them unto the adoption of children.

And yet, who in all honesty can claim for a moment that this greatest of all predestinarians was not on fire for the Lord? Did he not cry, "Woe is unto me if I do not preach the gospel of Jesus Christ, for necessity is laid upon me"? In fact, wasn't the very knowledge which Paul had through his vision, that the Lord had much people in Corinth, the stimulus he needed to remain in that city for one and a half years to labor diligently in order that those people whom the Lord had there might hear the gospel and be saved? Do the constant statements of Paul to the effect that he prayed for the newly founded churches day and night without ceasing sound as though election had dampened his spirits? Do not his labors of three years in Ephesus with tears reveal the spirit of a man who cannot do enough for the Lord? Wasn't it Paul who said that he did not hold his life of any account just so long as he could testify of the grace of God? Would you consider one to have no zeal for the cause who

---

[7]Stickelberger, p. 148.

was beaten three times with a rod, once stoned, three times shipwrecked; who spent twenty-four hours in the deep; who was in journeyings often, in perils of rivers, in perils of robbers, in perils of his countrymen, in perils from the Gentiles, in perils in the city, in perils in the wilderness, in perils in the sea, in labor and travail, in watchings often, in hunger and thirst, in fastings often, in cold and nakedness? Is that a cold, frigid, heartless, quenched spirit without zeal or initiative?

You see, the Bible and the very history of the church belie those opinions which accuse Calvinism of being a deadening influence — something that should be hidden and not talked about and only thought of when no one is around.

Instead, therefore, of dreading the great truths of the sovereignty of God, let us be ecstatic in our gratitude to God for His predestinating love, which, in spite of every man's utter rebellion against God and hatred toward Him, was bent on saving some to the uttermost. And let us thank God that even our faith is from Him and was given to us in an irresistible way. For we know that we are by nature so depraved that if God had not worked in His irresistibly winsome way, we would never have believed. Moreover, thanks be to God that Christ did not die in some insipid, weak way for all men, so that the salvation of no one was certain, but its realization was left up to the totally depraved. But thank God that Christ's death was an absolute guarantee that every single one of the elect would be saved. And once saved, let us thank God that we do not have to tremble for fear that tomorrow we might become apostate and be eternally lost, but rather, that once saved, we will always be saved. In other words, "Blessed be the God and Father of our Lord Jesus Christ, who hath blessed us with every spiritual blessing in the heavenly places in Christ: even as he chose us in him before the foundation of the world, that we should be holy and without blemish before him in love: having foreordained us unto adoption as sons through Jesus Christ unto himself, according to the good pleasure of his will, to the praise of the glory of his grace, which he freely bestowed on us in the Beloved" (Eph. 1:3-6).

And, finally, do not forget to make "your calling and election sure" (II Peter 1:10). For it is possible for you to know all about predestination and yet go to hell, all because you do not sincerely go to Jesus in repentance and ask Him to save you from your sins. So, in the name of God, I command and invite you: believe on the Lord Jesus Christ. It's up to you.

But if you do believe, then thank God for making you want to believe.

Soli Deo gratia: To God alone be the thanks.

DISCUSSION QUESTIONS

1. Read the Conclusion of the Canons of Dort and discuss two ideas that were new to you.
2. In their Conclusion, the Canons of Dort deny the following:
   a. that God is "the Author of sin";
   b. "in the same manner in which the election is the fountain and cause of faith and good works, reprobation is the cause of unbelief and impiety."
   Discuss these statements.
3. Is everything ordained by God? Prove your answer from the Bible.
4. If sin is not ordained by God, name the human actions and historical events that are.
5. Turn in your Bibles to the following passages and discuss what they say about sin being ordained by God:
   a. Genesis 45:5-8
   b. Genesis 50:20
   c. Acts 2:23
   d. Acts 4:28
6. Likewise, look up the following Bible verses and discuss what they say about God ordaining sin:
   a. Joshua 11:20
   b. I Samuel 16:23
   c. II Samuel 12:11-12
   d. II Samuel 16:10-11
   e. I Kings 22:20-33
   f. Job 1:21
   g. Isaiah 10:5
   h. II Thessalonians 2:11
   i. Revelation 17:17
7. Look up the following verses that indicate the holiness of God:
   a. Psalm 5:4-6
   b. Isaiah 6:3
   c. Romans 9:14
   d. I Peter 1:16
   e. Revelation 15:4
   How do you reconcile these with the Bible verses in questions 5 and 6?

8. How can a holy, omnipotent God ordain the Fall, sin, and hell?
9. Is it Biblical to say, "Salvation is up to you"?
10. How does the story of the shipwreck on Paul's journey show both divine sovereignty and human responsibility (Acts 27:22-25, 31)?
11. How does the Arminian impose a rationalistic logic on the Bible?
12. How does the hyper-Calvinist do it?
13. What stand does the Calvinist take in reference to these two extremes?
14. Is the "Predestinated Thief" to blame?
15. In deciding whether the Five Points of Calvinism are true or not, what must be our final and only authority? Why?
16. Turn to Deuteronomy 29:29 and explain it fully.
17. Read and discuss passages in the Bible that tell of the incomprehensibility of God, such as Isaiah 55:8-9, Job 38, and Romans 11:33-36. What are some others?
18. Would you like to know all God knows and be like Him? Be honest and say why.
19. How does Colossians 3:12 tie in divine sovereignty with human responsibility?
20. How does I Thessalonians 5:8-9 do it?
21. And II Thessalonians 2:13, 15?
22. Sometimes it is said that to teach that God foreordains all things kills all of man's initiative. How would you refute this argument from the lives of Paul and Calvin?
23. Why should you have tremendous joy and comfort in the last four points of the Five Points of Calvinism? Discuss them one at a time.
24. Tell what Article XIV of the Belgic Confession says about the following:
    a. sin in the plan of God
    b. God as the author of sin
    c. the proper attitude toward God's incomprehensible ways
    d. the comfort that God's foreordination brings

7

twelve theses on reprobation

Definition: Reprobation is God's eternal, sovereign, unconditional, immutable, wise, holy, and mysterious decree whereby, in electing some to eternal life, He passes others by, and then justly condemns them for their own sin—all to His own glory.

TWELVE THESES

1. The Bible is the infallible, inerrant Word of God and is the final arbiter in all teaching, including reprobation.
2. God is holy; He is the absolute antithesis of sin, and a hater of evil.
3. Although sin and unbelief are contrary to what God commands (His preceptive will), God has included them in His sovereign decree (ordained them, caused them to certainly come to pass).
4. Historically, many, but not all, theologians have spoken of two parts of reprobation: 1) preterition and 2) condemnation.
5. Reprobation as preterition is unconditional, and as condemnation it is conditional.
6. Preterition is the reverse side of election.
7. God does not effectuate sin and unbelief in the same way He effectuates good deeds and faith.
8. Objections to the teaching of reprobation are usually based on scholastic rationalism rather than on humble submission to the Word of God.
9. It is wrong to expect the Bible to give a systematic theological treatise of reprobation.
10. A person does not know if he is reprobate, but he may know if he is elect.
11. Reprobation should be preached.
12. Ignorance is wisdom.

THESIS 1

The Bible is the infallible, inerrant Word of God and is the final arbiter in all teaching, including reprobation.

Reprobation deals with divine mysteries that are unfathomable. At the outset the Christian must decide what is going to determine the answers to the question of reprobation: his finite, sinful mind or God's infallible Word, which is true in all parts and in all details. This question must be settled at the outset, for the Bible sets forth some mind-boggling truths.

THESIS 2

God is holy: He is the absolute antithesis of sin, and a hater of evil.

This is supported in the following:

a. Express declarations that God is holy:
   Lev. 11:44, 45; 19:2; 20:26.
   I Peter 1:16: "Be holy, because I am holy."[1]
   Joshua 24:19: "He is a holy God."
   I Samuel 2:2: "There is no one holy like the LORD."
   Psalm 99:5: "Exalt the LORD our God . . . he is holy."
   Isaiah 6:3: "Holy, holy, holy is the LORD Almighty."
   John 17:11: "Holy Father."

b. God commands holiness, thus reflecting His true nature.
   1. God gave the Ten Commandments.
   2. The prophets repeatedly stress holiness.
   3. Christ commands holiness.
   4. The New Testament writers stress holiness.

c. God punishes sin.
   In the Old and the New Testament, people are punished for their sins. Eternal hell exists because of man's lack of holiness.

d. God rewards holiness.
   Luke 6:35: "But love your enemies . . . Then your reward will be great . . ."
   I Corinthians 3:8: "Each will be rewarded according to his own labor."

e. God punished Christ in the place of sinners. It was because God is holy that He could not allow sin to go unpunished if people

---

[1] All Scripture quotations are from the *New International Version*.

were to go to heaven. So He punished Christ to make His chosen ones holy.

THESIS 3

Although sin and unbelief are contrary to what God commands (His preceptive will), God has included them in His sovereign decree (ordained them to certainly come to pass).

Before reading further, one must be absolutely sure of the first thesis, for this third thesis goes right to the heart of the problem.

Many Christians—who have not had time to think the matter through carefully, and even some who have—cannot bear to think that God has ordained sin. It sounds nonsensical, especially after the second thesis that God is holy and the antithesis of sin. How is it possible that a holy God, who hates sin, not only passively permits sin but also certainly and efficaciously decrees that sin shall be? This does not make sense, and so, without examining Scripture, they overthrow this third thesis as contradictory to the second one. Their logic, and not Scripture, has become the final arbiter of the truth of reprobation. This is why it is very important to make sure that the first thesis is believed. Our infinite God presents us with some astounding truths—truths that our sinful and finite minds rebel against.

Before presenting Biblical evidence that sin is not outside the sovereign, decretive will of God, note exactly what is being asserted:

a. All things that happen in all the world at any time and in all history—whether with inorganic matter, vegetation, animals, man, or angels (both the good and evil ones)—come to pass because God ordained them. Even sin—the fall of the devil from heaven, the fall of Adam, and every evil thought, word, and deed in all of history, including the worst sin of all, Judas' betrayal of Christ—is included in the eternal decree of our holy God.

If sin were outside of God's decree, then very little would be included in this decree. All the great empires would have been outside of God's eternal, determinative decrees, for they were built on greed, hate, and selfishness, not for the glory of the Triune God. Certainly the following rulers, who influenced world history and countless numbers of lives, did not carry out the expansion of their empires for the glory of God: Pharaoh, Nebuchadnezzar, Cyrus,

Alexander the Great, Ghenghis Khan, Caesar, Nero, Charles V, Henry VIII, Napoleon, Bismarck, Hitler, Stalin, Hirohito.

If sin were beyond the foreordination of God, then not only were these vast empires and their events outside God's plan, but also all the little daily events of every non-Christian are outside of God's power. For whatever is not done to the glory of the Christian God and out of faith in Jesus Christ is sin. Giving a million dollars to a hospital is certainly better than killing people, but if it is not done out of the proper motive of glorifying God, it is still rooted in sin.

The acts of the Christian are not perfect—even after he is born again and Christ is living in him. Sin still clings to him; he is not perfect until he is in heaven. For example, he does not love God with all of his heart, mind, and soul, nor does he truly love his neighbor as himself. Even his most admirable deeds are colored by sin.

It is true that God restrains the sin of the unbeliever and encourages him to do good and that the Holy Spirit also enables the Christian to do good. But if sin is outside the decree of God, then the vast percentage of human actions—both the trivial and the significant—are removed from God's plan. God's power is reduced to the forces of nature, such as the spinning of the galaxies and the laws of gravity and entropy. Most of history is outside His control.

Armies conquer, rulers are assassinated, empires rise and fall, but God has little to do with it if sin is outside His eternal decrees. The Moslems sweep over Africa and the Middle East and affect all of history, but this is not according to God's will—if sin is outside the plan of God.

b. Sin comes about by the efficacious permission of God, to use Augustine's term (*permissio efficax*). Augustine did not want to imply that God was an unholy God. So he said that sin was permitted by God. By this term he wanted to get God off the hook. He did not want to blame God. He wanted to indicate that sin is disobedience to God's commands (His preceptive will).

Yet he realized that simply to say God permits sin is contrary to God's sovereignty and would make Him a bystander in the bleachers, watching to see how the events on history's playing field turn out. So Augustine said that the permission is efficacious. This was his way of explaining both the second and third theses of this chapter. God permits sin; thus man is to blame and not God. But God *efficaciously* permits sin: Sin is not only foreknown by God, it is also foreordained by God. In fact, because God foreordained it, He foreknew it.

Calvin is very clear on this point. "Man wills with an evil will what God wills with a good will."[2] Evil, "which is in itself contrary to the will of God, is not done without the will of God, because without God's will it could not have been done at all."[3] "To turn all those passages of Scripture . . . into a mere permission on the part of God is a frivolous subterfuge, and a vain attempt at escape from a mighty truth."[4]

Calvin approvingly quotes Augustine: "In a wonderful and ineffable way, that is not done without His will which is even done contrary to His will, because it could not have been done had He not permitted it to be done; and yet, He did not permit it without His will, but according to His will."[5]

To say it in another way, God willingly permits sin. To be sure, God hates sin and does not desire it. Furthermore, He sincerely desires the salvation of all. He does not want "anyone to perish, but everyone to come to repentance" (II Peter 3:9). In this sense God unwillingly permits sin. It is against His holy nature and His revealed will. On the other hand, God willingly permits sin in that it is in accordance with His decree and not outside of His sovereign will.

To speak of God efficaciously permitting sin may not appreciably help our understanding. It is a feeble attempt to describe what the Bible says. In the final analysis, we cannot really understand. When it comes to these deepest of divine mysteries, we stumble and stutter. All we can do is to parrot the Bible.

Already we parroted the Bible about God's holiness (Thesis 2). Now all we can do is to parrot the Bible in asserting that sin is not outside the divine decree but has been foreordained by a holy, loving, wise God. We may not be able to reconcile the two theses, but it is important to state them and give the Biblical data.

Here is some of the Biblical evidence. (Further evidence is given in the appendix of this chapter.) It is not necessary to read all the evidence. The reader can dip in here and there to see what the Bible says. But it is important to cite many Biblical passages, because it would diminish the effect of the argument to cite just some representative cases, as was done with God's holiness (Thesis 2). The Bible has well over a hundred examples in which God brought

[2]John Calvin, *Calvin's Calvinism* (Grand Rapids: Wm. B. Eerdmans Publishing Co., 1950), p. 196.
[3]Calvin, *Calvin's Calvinism*, p. 200.
[4]Calvin, *Calvin's Calvinism*, p. 201.
[5]Calvin, *Calvin's Calvinism*, p. 253.

sin to pass. The following list is fairly large, but it is by no means complete.

1. Acts 2:23

"This man [Jesus] was handed over to you by God's set purpose and foreknowledge."

Here Peter explicitly states that the sinful betrayal and killing of Jesus was brought to pass by God's set purpose. The death of Christ was not left to chance. The salvation of the believer by the substitutionary atonement of Christ on the cross was no accident; it was not left to the arbitrary whim of the people. Nobody could be saved without the substitutionary death of Jesus. If the crowds, the priests, and the soldiers had not conspired to kill Him, then there would have been no salvation, no divine election, no church, no heaven. God would have been frustrated.

But the Bible tells us that this most evil of all sins—the crucifixion of Jesus—came about by "God's set purpose." Sin and unbelief were ordained by God.

Notice the juxtaposition between God's ordination of sin and man's blame. The first part of the verse ("handed over to you by God's set purpose") clearly teaches that God decrees sin; but right in the same breath, in the same sentence, the Bible puts all the blame on man. Our logic would tell us to blame God. He did it; it is His fault. But it was the Holy Spirit who inspired Peter to say, "And you, with the help of wicked men, put him to death by nailing him to the cross." Wicked men—they were to blame.

This is the awesome Biblical asymmetry: God ordains sin, and man is to blame. We cannot comprehend this. We can only come back to the first thesis: "The Bible is the infallible, inerrant Word of God and is the final arbiter in all teaching, including reprobation."

2. Acts 4:27, 28

"Indeed Herod and Pontius Pilate met together with the Gentiles and the people of Israel in this city to conspire against your holy servant Jesus, whom you anointed. They did what your power and will had decided beforehand should happen."

These verses closely parallel Acts 2:23 in that they speak of the death of Jesus as being foreordained by God. Again there is the juxtaposition of man's blame and God's decree. By quoting the second Psalm, Peter reproaches Herod, Pontius Pilate, the Gentiles, and the people of Israel for Christ's death ("nations rage . . . peoples plot . . . against the Lord and against his Anointed One," Acts 4:25, 26).

At the same time Peter says that this sin was what God's "power and will had decided beforehand should happen." Peter could have said that they merely did what God "had decided" should happen. That would have been very clear. Herod did not decide. God decided. But Peter strengthens this clear statement:

a. He says, God "decided beforehand." The word *beforehand* stresses that the sin was in God's hands and not in the rulers' and Gentiles'.
b. It would have been enough to say that God "decided beforehand." But Peter places further emphasis on God's sovereignty by saying, His "will" decided, instead of saying, "God" decided.
c. Peter adds a third touch: Instead of saying that God had decided beforehand or even God's will had decided beforehand, he adds "power" to the "will."

It is impossible for anyone to say on the basis of the Bible that the sinful killing of Jesus—and that also means unbelief—was not ordained by God. The Scriptures are most emphatic.

3. *Acts 3:18*

"But this is how God fulfilled what he had foretold through all the prophets, saying that his Christ would suffer."

Just prior to this verse Peter rebuked and blamed the Jews for killing Jesus: "You handed him over to be killed, and you disowned him before Pilate—You disowned the Holy and Righteous One and asked that a murderer be released to you. You killed the author of life." But Peter goes on to say that this was how God fulfilled what had been prophesied about the death of Christ.

So, who did it? Who killed Jesus? The Bible says that the Jews did. They were to blame. Yet in the very next breath it says that God was the one who fulfilled what had already been prophesied about Christ's death.

All things, including sin, are brought to pass by God—without God violating His holiness. (Notice again the placing side by side of man's guilt and God's ordination of sin.)

4. *Luke 22:22*

"The Son of Man will go as it has been decreed, but woe to that man who betrays him."

In this verse "will go" refers to what had just been said, namely, that Judas would betray Jesus. So Jesus was saying with the utmost clarity that the future events in His life—the betrayal, trial, and crucifixion—had "been decreed." They were unchangeable. God had determined them. In other words, God ordained sin and unbelief.

Again, there is a sharp juxtaposition of divine sovereignty and human responsibility. In the very same sentence in which Jesus said that His betrayal had been decreed, He concluded, "But woe to that man who betrays him."

Man always recoils at this juxtaposition. He wants to say that either God is sovereign and man is not responsible; or he wants to assert man's responsibility and take away God's sovereignty. However, the Bible repeatedly puts the two side by side. It is the Christian's duty to accept both, recognizing that God's thoughts are higher than man's thoughts, as the heavens are higher than the earth.

5. Genesis 45:5-8

"And now, do not be distressed and do not be angry with yourselves for selling me here, because it was to save lives that God sent me ahead of you. For two years now there has been famine in the land, and for the next five years there will not be plowing and reaping. But God sent me ahead of you to preserve for you a remnant on earth and to save your lives by a great deliverance. So then, it was not you who sent me here, but God." (See also Psalm 105:17.)

This passage is one of Scripture's most powerful statements in support of God's power over man's sin. In fact, it is so strikingly clear that it cannot easily be misinterpreted. Notice God's role in the events of Joseph's life.

a. Joseph almost excused his brothers for their dastardly crime. They were wrong, they acted immorally, they hated their brother and planned to kill him. In actuality they sold him into slavery, and then they concocted a story and blatantly lied to their father. Yet Joseph is saying, "Don't worry; God was in back of it all."

b. Yet Joseph said that they did not send him into Egypt. How could he say this? Chapter 37 clearly states that "they plotted to kill him" (v. 18) and they "sold him for twenty shekels of silver" (v. 28). Joseph knew this only too well through personal experience. In 45:8, when he said right out, "It was not you who sent me here," he was not contradicting what he knew very well,

namely, that they did send him to Egypt. But this was just his
way of pointing out that the sin of his brothers was not something
that happened haphazardly, by chance, without God having anything to do with it. In some mysterious way God, who is absolutely holy and who hates sin, was deeply involved in the sin of
Joseph's brothers.

The reason was that God wanted to preserve Israel as a nation. He
did not want it to be wiped out by the upcoming famine. For God
had plans: He wanted "to save lives," the lives of the Israelites. He
wanted "to preserve . . . a remnant on earth and to save . . . lives."
The Bible does not say it here, but God also wanted to have a people
out of whom would come the Messiah, the Savior of the world.

God was not going to leave this plan to chance, to the will of men.
So Joseph makes the astounding statement that his brothers did not
send him into Egypt! Well, if they did not commit this sin, who did?

"God sent me" (45:5). In case there were still any lingering doubts
as to who was in back of this heinous crime, the Bible comes out
clearly and says that it was God! Nothing could be clearer: "So then,
it was not you who sent me here, but God."

I almost recoil in writing this. Selling Joseph into slavery was a
criminal act. It involved murderous plotting, betrayal, and deceitfulness. Yet who did that? "It was not you who sent me here, but
God." This is why the first two theses were introduced first: The
Bible is true, and God is holy. We must never forget this.

6. Genesis 50:19, 20

"But Joseph said to them, 'Don't be afraid. Am I in the place of
God? You intended to harm me, but God intended it for good to
accomplish what is now being done, the saving of many lives."

What is so striking here is that the same verb is used in reference
to the actions of God as to the evil, sinful actions of Joseph's brothers
(*intend*). Joseph's brothers intended evil when they sold Joseph.
Now God, of course, intended the opposite in order that Israel
might be saved. But regardless of His motive, the fact is that in
some way that is not clear to us, God, who abhors sin, actively used
sin to accomplish His purpose. Joseph's brothers intended and God
intended. The same verb for the same actions, but with different
motives.

The rest of the Biblical evidence for this astounding third thesis is
found in the appendix. But the Bible is clear: God ordains sin.

THESIS 4

Historically, many, but not all, theologians have spoken of two parts of reprobation: 1) preterition and 2) condemnation.

1. *Preterition* (from the Latin *praeter* [by] + *ire* [to go]) means to *pass by*. In decreeing that some should be saved, God chose (elected) some people and passed others by.
2. *Condemnation.* Those who are passed by are condemned eternally for their sins.

Other theologians prefer to restrict reprobation only to preterition. This parallels election more closely. But it makes no difference at all—whether or not condemnation is included—as long as what is meant by the term *reprobation* is clear.

THESIS 5

Reprobation as preterition is unconditional, and as condemnation it is conditional.

1. Preterition is unconditional.

God's passing some by was not conditioned by their unbelief. God did not foresee which ones by their own will would not accept Christ, and on that basis reject them. Just as election is unconditional (God did not choose anybody because He foresaw they would believe in Jesus), so also is preterition unconditional. It is no more based on God's foreknowledge of what an independent human being would do with Jesus than is election. As the reason for election is found in God alone—and never in man—so also is the reason for preterition found in God alone and not in man.

The only reason given for the election of Jacob and the passing by of Esau is: "Jacob I loved, but Esau I hated" (Rom. 9:13). The reason was in God and not in the foreknowledge of the good or bad that either one would do. ("Before the twins were born or had done anything good or bad—in order that God's purpose in election might stand: not by works but by him who called—she was told, 'The older will serve the younger.'") As Calvin said, "As Jacob, deserving nothing by good works, is taken into grace, so Esau, as yet undefiled by any crime, is hated."[6]

---

[6]John Calvin, *Institutes of the Christian Religion*, 3.22.11.

The most powerful evidence that preterition is unconditional and that unbelief is ordained by God is found in the hypothetical questions that Paul raises in response to this strong assertion of God's sovereignty in both election and reprobation. He asks hypothetically, as if a doubter were questioning God's wisdom: "What then shall we say? Is God unjust?" This question presupposes that double predestination (election and reprobation) is unconditional, that it is not based on God's foreknowledge of who would believe or not, who would be good or evil. For if predestination were based on what God foresaw man would believe or do, then predestination would seem to be completely fair. Man would then get what he deserves. And there would be no need for Paul to raise these questions.

So the very question about God's unfairness ("Is God unjust?") necessarily presupposes that election and reprobation are not based on what man does, but on God's decree.

As a matter of fact, Paul immediately goes on to say just that. "For he says to Moses, 'I will have mercy on whom I have mercy, and I will have compassion on whom I have compassion.' It does not, therefore, depend on man's desire or effort, but on God's mercy" (Rom. 9:15, 16).

Paul follows up by reasserting that "God has mercy on whom he wants to have mercy, and he hardens whom he wants to harden" (Rom. 9:18). Again he asks a question: "One of you will say to me: 'Then why does God still blame us? For who resists his will?'"

Again, these very questions can be understood only if preterition and unbelief are grounded in God. For if preterition and unbelief were grounded ultimately in man—if God condemned to hell only those who He foresaw would reject Jesus, apart from any influence from God—then there would be no reason for Paul to raise this hypothetical question about blame. The blame would be squarely on man, and Paul would not question God's fairness. The question of inequity makes sense only on the basis of what Paul had just said, namely, that election and reprobation do not "depend on man's desire (belief or unbelief) or effort" and that God "hardens whom he wants to harden."

Thus, Romans 9 is clear in asserting that both election and preterition are unconditional. Their ultimate foundation is in God: "Jacob I loved, but Esau I hated."

2. Condemnation is conditional.

Reprobation as condemnation is conditional in the sense that once someone is passed by, then he is condemned by God for his sins and unbelief. Although all things—unbelief and sin included—proceed from God's eternal decree, man is still to blame for his sins. He is guilty; it is his fault and not God's.

THESIS 6

Preterition is the reverse side of election.

If God chooses some, then He necessarily passes others by. Up implies down; back implies front; wet implies dry; later implies earlier; choosing implies leaving others unchosen.

To say this is not a misuse of logic, but a necessity in speaking. To choose some—by very definition of the Biblical term itself—means that some were not chosen, that some were left behind, that some were passed by. To choose sixty apples out of one hundred means that forty were left behind. It is impossible to select or elect some without leaving others unselected.

Instead of preterition being a logical deduction from election, as some would have us believe, preterition is in the very definition of Biblical, divine election. Election without preterition is theological gobbledygook, a mythical inanity of an uncritical mind.

As Calvin said, "Indeed, many, as if they wished to avert a reproach from God, accept election in such terms as to deny that anyone is condemned. But they do this very ignorantly and childishly, since election itself could not stand except as set over against reprobation."[7]

THESIS 7

God does not effectuate sin and unbelief in the same way He effectuates good deeds and faith.

All things and events are ordained by God. His decree effectually brings about everything. But God does not work in the same direct way in reprobation as in election. Nor does God delight in the sin He foreordains in the same way He delights in the good He foreordains. In the one He wills unwillingly and in the other willingly. As Calvin said, "Although God and the devil will the same thing, they do so in an entirely different manner."[8]

---

[7]Calvin, *Institutes*, 3.23.1.
[8]Calvin, *Calvin's Calvinism*, p. 196.

In the one case God delights in sending the Holy Spirit, but in the ordaining of the devil and sin He finds no pleasure. In the one case God sends His Holy Spirit to live in people and to establish a spiritual union between them and Christ; but in the case of the reprobate God does not send the devil to dwell in them and to establish a spiritual union between them and the devil. Although the Holy Spirit is the fountain from whom faith and holiness immediately arise, there is no counterpart in the devil, no parallel fountain that produces unbelief and evil.

The Canons of Dort (1619) were clear in rejecting the idea "that in the same manner in which election is the fountain and cause of faith and good works, reprobation is the cause of unbelief and impiety." (It should be carefully noted that the Canons do not deny that God decrees unbelief and impiety; they only deny that the manner of the decree is similar.)

THESIS 8

Objections to the teaching of reprobation are usually based on scholastic rationalism rather than on humble submission to the Word of God.

As usual, the Arminian and the denier of reprobation reason: It is ridiculous to say that God has ordained all things—including unbelief and hell—for then God is the author of sin, and man is not to blame. He writes: "How can the God of truth, who daily keeps covenant in nature and in grace, sincerely and in good faith call men to believe in Him and accept the gospel when in actual fact He has by an eternal decree forever determined that they will, under no circumstances, be able to accept the call when it comes to them? How can you read it other than as a total contradiction, a yes and a no on the same point?"

The question that is being asked is not: What does the Bible say? But rather: What can my finite reason understand? What is contradictory and what is not?

How different this is from Calvin's humbler approach to the Word of God! He accepts everything in the Bible, even if it is beyond his comprehension and reason. "Monstrous indeed is the madness of men, who desire thus to subject the immeasurable to the puny measure of their own reason!"[9]

---

[9]Calvin, *Institutes*, 3.23.4.

In his *Consensus Genevensis*, after asserting firmly that sin is in the eternal decree of God, Calvin says: "If anyone should reply that this is above the capability of his mind to comprehend, I also acknowledge and confess the same. But why should we wonder that the infinite and incomprehensible majesty of God should surpass the narrow limits of our finite intellect? So far, however, am I from undertaking to explain this sublime and hidden mystery by any powers of human reason, that I would ever retain in my own memory what I declared at the commencement of this discussion—that those who seek to know more than God has revealed are madmen! Wherefore, let us delight ourselves more in wise ignorance than in an immoderate and intoxicated curiosity to know more than God permits."[10]

Or elsewhere: "As soon as a reason cannot be immediately seen for certain works of God, men somehow or other are immediately prepared to appoint a day for entering into judgment with Him."[11]

Further: "How it was that God by His foreknowledge and decree ordained what should take place respecting man, and yet so ordained it without His being Himself in the least a participator of the fault, or being at all the author or the approver of the transgression—how this was, I repeat, is a secret manifestly far too deep to be penetrated by the human mind, nor am I ashamed to confess his ignorance of that which the Lord envelops in the blaze of His own inaccessible light."[12]

Thus Calvin acknowledges that the decree of sin and reprobation is far beyond his understanding, but he humbly accepts the decrees because God has so revealed them. "Ignorance that believes is better than rash knowledge."[13]

John Murray also takes this same humble attitude toward the Word of God, even though to his mind there is a "contradiction."[14] "And there is a *disparity* between the decretive will and the preceptive will, between the determinations of his secret counsel that certain events will come to pass and the prescriptions of his revealed will to us that we do not bring these events to pass. It cannot be gainsaid that God decretively forbids what he preceptively commands. It is precisely in this consideration that the doctrine of God's

---

[10]Calvin, *Calvin's Calvinism*, p. 127.
[11]Calvin, *Calvin's Calvinism*, p. 32.
[12]Calvin, *Calvin's Calvinism*, p. 128.
[13]Calvin, *Institutes*, 3.23.5.
[14]John Murray, *Calvin on Scripture and Divine Sovereignty* (Grand Rapids: Baker Book House, 1960), p. 69.

sovereignty is focused most acutely with its demands for our faith and reverence. If I am not mistaken, it is at this point that the sovereignty of God makes the human mind reel as it does nowhere else in connection with this topic."[15]

Our attitude to this great mystery of reprobation and the love of God should be like Paul's when he said, "Who are you, O man, to talk back to God? 'Shall what is formed say to him who formed it, "Why did you make me like this?"'" (Rom. 9:20). And, "Oh, the depth of the riches of the wisdom and knowledge of God! How unsearchable his judgments, and his paths beyond tracing out!" (Rom. 11:33).

When God speaks—as He has clearly done in Romans 9—then we are simply to follow and believe, even if we cannot understand, and even if it seems to be a contradiction to our puny minds.

THESIS 9

It is wrong to expect the Bible to give a systematic theological treatise of reprobation.

Some disparage the Biblical teaching of reprobation because there are not many texts dealing with it and because it is not neatly and systematically set forth in one section.

Such disparagement arises from naiveté. The purpose of the Bible is not to give a systematic presentation of doctrines. Its goal is to show a person how to be saved and how to live. However, by comparing Scripture with Scripture it is possible, at times, to arrive at a fairly full description of those facts. Thus, there is no one place that gives us in a neat package all the data about the Trinity or the natures of Christ à la Chalcedon, but the facts are there.

And sometimes logic—to the dismay of some Biblicists—has to be used. But there is nothing wrong with using reason and logic if we do it properly. There is a correct and an incorrect way of doing that. For example, there is no place in the Bible that says the Christian should baptize infants; yet this necessary practice can be deduced from the Scriptures. The basis for infant baptism is found in the data of Scripture. Nor is there any place that says women are allowed to partake of the Lord's Supper, and yet this can also be deduced from Scripture. In fact, it is desirable to do so.

---

[15]Murray, *Calvin on Scripture and Divine Sovereignty*, p. 68.

So, likewise, there is no one place that spells out in a systematic, theological way that there are two parts to reprobation, that reprobation is the necessary counterpart to election, that from eternity God foreordained some to unbelief and hell, that the sinner and not God is to blame, and that the sinner will be condemned for his own sins. Yet, just as surely as the church practices infant baptism, so also does it teach the truth of reprobation.

THESIS 10

A person does not know if he is reprobate, but he may know if he is elect.

There is no way for anyone to know if he is eternally lost, for there is always the possibility that he may turn to Christ up until the time he dies.

On the other side, it is possible for a person to know if he is elect. If he sincerely believes on Jesus Christ, then he knows he is saved. John writes, "I write these things to you who believe in the name of the Son of God so that you may know that you have eternal life" (I John 5:13). And if a person is saved, then he is elect, for it is God who chose him to be saved (II Thess. 2:13) and predestined him to be adopted as His son (Eph. 1:5).

A church may never exercise excommunication on the basis of reprobation, for the church never knows who is reprobate. Rather, the church must always invite all sinners to Christ—even the excommunicated! It exercises church discipline only on the basis of unrepentance, never on some secret, divine knowledge about who is elect and who is reprobate.

THESIS 11

Reprobation should be preached.

Some shy away from preaching on reprobation, but only because of ignorance. No one should ever consider himself wiser than God and keep hidden what God has revealed. Rather, he should follow Paul's example at Ephesus, when he said that he did not hesitate to proclaim "the whole will of God" (Acts 20:27).

Calvin said it plainly: "Therefore we must be on our guard against depriving believers of anything disclosed about predestination in

Scripture, lest we seem either wickedly to defraud them of the blessing of their God or to accuse and scoff at the Holy Spirit for having published what it is in any way profitable to suppress."[16]

A good rule of thumb is to give to reprobation and election the same emphasis and proportion that the Bible gives. Naturally the Bible does not put a great amount of stress on the devil, hell, and reprobation. But it does teach them and so should the Bible-believing Christian. The heart of the Bible is the good news of a Savior, heaven, and election. The message of salvation is on every page, and should be stressed accordingly.

THESIS 12

Ignorance is wisdom.

When dealing with the foreordination of sin and unbelief, human responsibility, reprobation, and God's holiness, we come into some of the deepest mysteries of all eternity. These are not issues like the secrets of the universe, where often we can say, "Only give me tomorrow and I will plumb the depths of the universe." Rather we are dealing with mysteries that will not be solved today, or in a millennium, or in eternity. Even when we see God face to face, we will still be creatures with a finite understanding. His knowledge is not only quantitatively greater than ours, but also qualitatively distinctive from ours.

It is necessary, therefore, that we recognize the limits of our knowledge, that we do not pry into areas not revealed to us. As John Calvin said regarding these matters, "Ignorance is wisdom; the craving to know, a kind of madness,"[17] and, "Let us not be ashamed to be ignorant of something in this matter, wherein there is a certain wise ignorance."[18]

We return full circle to the first thesis: The Bible is the infallible and inerrant Word of God and is the final arbiter in all teaching, including reprobation. The temptation is to accept only what our logic approves rather than what the Bible teaches. Our minds reject the idea that a holy God can ordain unbelief and sin. But we must learn humility and accept what God has revealed. If the hundred

---

[16]Calvin, *Institutes*, 3.21.3.
[17]Calvin, *Institutes*, 3.23.8.
[18]Calvin, *Institutes*, 3.21.2.

cited texts—or even just one—reveal that God has ordained sin, then we must accept that on faith.

We should not profess ignorance where God has spoken. That too is disrespect for God. Everything that God reveals is profitable and should be examined. Thus, our goal in the teaching of reprobation should be to go just as far as the Bible does, but no further.

APPENDIX TO THESIS 3
(Sin and Unbelief Are Ordained by God)

1. Many passages speak of God hardening hearts.

Joshua 11:20
"For it was the LORD himself who hardened their hearts to wage war against Israel, so that he might destroy them totally, exterminating them without mercy, as the LORD had commanded Moses."

Deuteronomy 2:30
"But Sihon king of Heshbon refused to let us pass through. For the LORD your God had made his spirit stubborn and his heart obstinate in order to give him into your hands, as he has now done."

Exodus 4:21
"The LORD said to Moses, . . . 'I will harden [Pharaoh's] heart so that he will not let my people go.'" See also Exodus 7:3; 9:12; 10:1, 20, 27; 11:10; 14:4, 8, 17; Romans 9:18.

Now some think that God hardened the hearts of Pharaoh and Sihon after—not before—they became stubborn. However, Deuteronomy 2:30 says that Sihon's refusal was caused by God's hardening of their hearts. There is nothing in the text or context to suggest that God hardened them as a punishment for their own sins. But in any case, whether God hardened hearts as a punishment for their sins or not, God did cause them to be stubborn and obstinate. God caused their sin to come to pass.

2. Many other passages speak of God causing enemies of Israel to attack them. Regardless of the fact that Israel deserved to be punished, it remains true that the war, killing, plundering, and destruction of property by Israel's enemies was sin. And the Bible is very clear in countless places that it was God who incited them and caused the attack.

Judges 3:8
"So the LORD sold them (the Israelites) into the hands of Jabin." Six times, before God raised up a "judge" to save Israel, the Bible tells us that it was the LORD who "sold" or "delivered" Israel into the hands of their enemies (king of Moab, 3:12; king of Canaan, 4:2; Midianites, 6:1;

Philistines and Ammonites, 10:7; Philistines, 13:1). In each of these cases, the attack against and conquering of Israel was sin.

II Kings 24:2
"The LORD sent Babylonian, Aramean, Moabite and Ammonite raiders against him. He sent them to destroy Judah, in accordance with the word of the LORD proclaimed by his servants the prophets."

II Chronicles 28:5
"Therefore the LORD his God handed him over to the king of Aram. The Arameans defeated him and took many of his people as prisoners and brought them to Damascus."

II Chronicles 33:11
"So the LORD brought against them the army commanders of the king of Assyria, who took Manasseh prisoner, put a hook in his nose, bound him with bronze shackles and took him to Babylon."

Job 1:21
"The LORD gave and the LORD has taken away." How did the LORD take away from Job? He caused the Sabeans and Chaldeans to raid, kill, and plunder so that only two of Job's servants escaped (1:13–15, 17).

Isaiah 5:25–29
"Therefore the LORD's anger burns against his people; his hand is raised and he strikes them down. . . . He lifts up a banner for the distant nations, he whistles for those at the ends of the earth. Here they come, swiftly and speedily! . . . Their roar is like that of the lion, they roar like young lions; they growl as they seize their prey and carry it off with none to rescue."

Isaiah 10:5, 6
God says: Assyria is "the rod of my anger, in whose hand is the club of my wrath! I send him against a godless nation, I dispatch him against a people who anger me, to seize loot and snatch plunder, and to trample them down like mud in the streets." In other words, the looting, plundering, and trampling is by God's decree. He "sends" the Assyrians, who acted in a sinful way.

It must not be thought that since Israel was disobedient, it was all right for the Assyrians to attack, plunder, and kill. It would not be in line with the Bible to say that we may do evil to carry out God's punishment. When God says that He will use the Assyrians as the rod of His anger, He puts the blame on the Assyrians by saying, "Woe to the Assyrian, the rod of my anger." God may have used the Assyrians to punish Israel, but Assyria sinned when it attacked God's people. This is the same kind of juxtaposition of human responsibility and divine ordination of sin that was earlier observed.

Jeremiah 12:12
"Therefore the LORD Almighty says this: 'Because you have not listened to my words, I will summon all the peoples of the north and my servant Nebuchadnezzar king of Babylon,' declares the LORD, 'and I will bring them against this land and its inhabitants and against all the

surrounding nations. I will completely destroy them and make them an object of horror and scorn, and an everlasting ruin. . . . This whole country will become a desolate wasteland, and these nations will serve the king of Babylon seventy years.' "

Such murderous rapine is a sin. It is done out of hate and selfishness, for self-glorification and not for the glory of God. As a matter of fact, the Bible has another one of those remarkable juxtapositions of God's sovereignty and man's responsibility. For right after saying, "I will summon. . . I will bring them against this land . . . I will completely destroy. . . I will banish," God puts the entire blame on the Babylonians: "But when the seventy years are fulfilled, I will punish the king of Babylon and his nation, the land of the Babylonians, for their guilt. . . . I will repay them according to their deeds and the work of their hands" (25:12–14).

How can God blame the Babylonians when He says that He summoned them to war? The Bible does not say. But it does clearly state that sin was not outside His plan.

Jeremiah 51:20–23
Speaking to the Babylonians, God says, "You are my war club, my weapon for battle—with you I shatter nations. . . kingdoms . . . horse and rider. . . chariot and driver. . . man and woman. . . old man and youth. . . young man and maiden. . . shepherd and flock. . . farmer and oxen. . . governors and officials."

Lamentations 1:17
"The LORD has decreed for Jacob that his neighbors become his foes." Note the word *decreed*.

Here is a partial list of Bible passages in which God said that He would cause some nations to attack Israel and other nations to attack the invaders: Exod. 33:2; I Kings 16:3; II Chron. 11:4; 12:8; 24:24; 25:16, 20; Isa. 44:28; 45:1; Jer. 1:15; 6:21; 11:11, 17; 22:5–8; 27:6–15; 28:14; 29:4, 17, 18, 21; 30:24; 32:23; 35:17; 42:10; 43:10–13; 44:6; 45:5; 46:15; 49:14; 52:3; Lam. 3:37, 38; Ezek. 12:15; 25:4–17; 28:17–19; 29:19, 20; 30:10–26; 32:12, 32; 35:10–15; 38:14–23; Hos. 1:4; Joel 3:7; Amos 3:6; 4:10, 11; 6:8, 11; Obad. 8 ff.; Mic. 2:3; 4:11, 12; 6:14, 16; Hab. 1:6, 12.

3. Several texts speak of God sending an evil or lying spirit that caused a person to sin. Yet God is a holy God who hates sin, and one person of the Trinity is the Holy Spirit, the antithesis of an evil spirit. The only explanation of these seemingly contradictory facts is that in some mysterious way God, without contradicting His holy nature, makes certain that these sins occur. He decrees that these specific sins shall be. Note the following texts:

Judges 9:22, 23
"After Abimelech had governed Israel three years, God sent an evil spirit between Abimelech and the citizens of Shechem, who acted treacherously against Abimelech. God did this in order that the crime against Jerub-Baal's seventy sons, the shedding of their blood, might be avenged. . . . "

I Samuel 16:14
"Now the Spirit of the LORD had departed from Saul, and an evil spirit from the LORD tormented him."

I Kings 22:23 and II Chronicles 18:21
"So now the LORD has put a lying spirit in the mouths of all these prophets of yours."

4. Certain texts speak of God's involvement in the lives of people who have fallen into sin.

I Samuel 2:25
Eli's sons were sleeping with prostitutes, for which Eli rebuked them. "His sons, however, did not listen to their father's rebuke, for it was the LORD's will to put them to death."

II Samuel 12:11, 12
David committed adultery with Bathsheba. God said that He would punish David in kind. "This is what the LORD says: 'Out of your own household I am going to bring calamity upon you. Before your very eyes I will take your wives and give them to one who is close to you, and he will lie with your wives in broad daylight. You did it in secret, but I will do this thing in broad daylight before all Israel.'" Note the strong words, "I will do this thing."

II Samuel 16:10
Shimei cursed David when David was fleeing. In response to a suggestion that David kill him, he absolved Shimei of the blame and said, "If he is cursing because the LORD said to him, 'Curse David,' who can ask, 'Why do you do this?'"

II Samuel 24:1 and I Chronicles 21:1
Chronicles says that "Satan rose up against Israel and incited David to take a census of Israel," whereas Samuel says that the Lord incited David. The same verb is used in both cases—*incited*. There are only two possible solutions to this seeming contradiction: 1) The Bible is in error (a Christian who believes that the Scriptures cannot be broken will not choose this escape); and 2) in God's inscrutable plan, without God's holiness being compromised, He used David's sinful action for His own purpose.

When the Bible says that God incited David, it must not be thought that God incites evil the same way he incites good. (See Thesis 8.) God does not tempt anyone (James 1:13). Nevertheless, it would not do justice to Scripture to say that God simply permitted Satan to incite David. Just as Christ's crucifixion was determined by God, so David's sin was determined by God. It was decreed by God. Nothing—not even Satan's evil plans—are outside the decrees of God.

As we have seen several times, when the Scriptures speak of God determining sin, they put the blame on man and not God. Thus in verse 10 David confesses that his census of Israel was his own sin: "David was conscience-stricken after he had counted the fighting men, and he said to the LORD, 'I have sinned greatly in what I have done. Now, O

LORD, I beg you, take away the guilt of your servant. I have done a very foolish thing.' " The punishments that David could choose from are listed in verses 12 and 13. The fact that punishment was necessary presupposes guilt on David's part.

Psalm 105:24, 25
"The LORD made his people very fruitful; he made them too numerous for their foes, whose hearts he turned to hate his people."

Proverbs 16:4
"The LORD works out everything for his own ends—even the wicked for a day of disaster."

II Thessalonians 2:11, 12
"For this reason God sends them a powerful delusion so that they will believe the lie and so that all will be condemned. . . ." Regardless of the reason, God did cause them to believe a lie. See also II Sam. 17:14; Ezek. 3:20; 14:9; Rev. 17:17.

It has been necessary in presenting the Biblical idea of reprobation to go to some length in drawing attention to these scores of texts that indicate sin is foreordained by God. The failure to believe this essential truth is one of the most common reasons that some do not believe in reprobation. If God has ordained only the good and pleasant things in life, then it is obvious that the unbelief of reprobation has not been foreordained. On the other hand, if all things are ordained by God—including sin and unbelief—then God has ordained who will be unbelievers. So, for the teaching of reprobation it is essential to establish the Biblical data on the foreordination of sin.

DISCUSSION QUESTIONS

1. Read the definition of reprobation again (p. 95) and tell how reprobation is: 1) eternal, 2) sovereign, 3) unconditional, 4) immutable, 5) wise, 6) holy, and 7) mysterious.
2. Is the Bible without error? Why do you think so?
3. Can the Bible be trusted in this difficult matter of reprobation?
4. Show from the Bible that God hates sin.
5. What is meant by God's preceptive will (will of His command) and His decretive will?
6. Some call God's decretive will His secret will. In what way is it secret and in what way is it not?
7. What does Deuteronomy 29:29 say about God's preceptive and decretive will?
8. What is preterition? Be sure you know the precise meaning of this term.
9. What is condemnation?
10. If you had to define reprobation, would you include condemnation in addition to preterition? Explain why.
11. What does it mean to say that preterition is unconditional? Can you prove it from the Bible?
12. Is election possible without preterition? Explain.
13. Explain this statement: God unwillingly wills sin.
14. Is it possible to say that God ordains sin without His being responsible for sin? Prove it.
15. What did Augustine mean when he said that God efficaciously permitted sin?
16. Should everything in the Bible be preached, including reprobation? Or only what the preacher thinks is edifying for the congregation?
17. How can you know if you are saved?
18. How can you know if you are reprobate? Are you sure of your answer?
19. What does it mean to say, "Ignorance is wisdom"?
20. What do the Heidelberg Catechism (p. 131) and the Belgic Confession (p. 121) say about God?

8

resource materials

Calvin's Attitude Toward Predestination

Calvin wrote that in dealing with predestination there are two attitudes that should be avoided: excessive curiosity in what God has not revealed and excessive timidity in teaching what He has revealed.

In the first case, "human curiosity renders the discussion of predestination, already somewhat difficult in itself, very confusing and even dangerous. No restraints can hold it back from wandering in forbidden bypaths and thrusting upward to the heights. If allowed, it will leave no secret to God that it will not search out and unravel. Since we see so many on all sides rushing into this audacity and impudence, among them certain men not otherwise bad, they should in due season be reminded of the measure of their duty in this regard.

"First, then, let them remember that when they inquire into predestination they are penetrating the sacred precincts of divine wisdom. If anyone with carefree assurance breaks into this place, he will not succeed in satisfying his curiosity and he will enter a labyrinth from which he can find no exit. For it is not right for man unrestrainedly to search out things that the Lord has willed to be hidden in himself; nor is it right for him to investigate from eternity that sublimest wisdom, which God would have us revere but not understand in order that through this also he should fill us with wonder. He has set forth by his Word the secrets of his will that he has decided to reveal to us. These he decided to reveal in so far as he foresaw that they would concern us and benefit us."[1]

For Calvin, the Word of God is the only norm for our dealing

---

[1]John Calvin, *Institutes of the Christian Religion*, III, xxi, 1.

with predestination. "If this thought prevails with us that the Word of the Lord is the sole way that can lead us in our search for all that it is lawful to hold concerning him, and is the sole light to illumine our vision of all that we should see of him, it will readily keep and restrain us from all rashness. For we shall know that the moment we exceed the bounds of the Word, our course is outside the pathway and in darkness, and that there we must repeatedly wander, slip, and stumble. Let this, therefore, first of all be before our eyes: to seek any other knowledge of predestination than what the Word of God discloses is not less insane than if one should purpose to walk in a pathless waste or to see in darkness. And let us not be ashamed to be ignorant of something in this matter, wherein there is a certain learned ignorance. Rather, let us willingly refrain from inquiring into a kind of knowledge, the ardent desire for which is both foolish and dangerous, nay, even deadly. But if a wanton curiosity agitates us, we shall always do well to oppose to it this restraining thought: just as too much honey is not good, so for the curious the investigation of glory is not turned into glory. For there is good reason for us to be deterred from this insolence which can plunge us into ruin."[2]

The second attitude that should be avoided, says Calvin, is that of those who "all but require that every mention of predestination be buried; indeed, they teach us to avoid any question of it, as we would a reef." This attitude is also wrong. "For Scripture is the school of the Holy Spirit, in which, as nothing is omitted that is both necessary and useful to know, so nothing is taught but what is expedient to know. Therefore we must guard against depriving believers of anything disclosed about predestination in Scripture, lest we seem either wickedly to defraud them of the blessing of their God or to accuse and scoff at the Holy Spirit for having published what it is in any way profitable to suppress. Let us, I say, permit the Christian man to open his mind and ears to every utterance of God directed to him, provided it be with such restraint that when the Lord closes his holy lips, he also shall at once close the way to inquiry."[3]

Calvin concludes his remarks by saying that he wishes that those who want to bury predestination would "admit that we

---

[2]Calvin, III, xxi, 2.
[3]Calvin, III, xxi, 3.

---

should not investigate what the Lord has left hidden in secret, that we should not neglect what he has brought into the open, so that we may not be convicted of excessive curiosity on the one hand, or of excessive ingratitude on the other. . . . Whoever, then, heaps odium upon the doctrine of predestination only reproaches God, as if God had unadvisedly let slip something hurtful to the church."[4]

Thus Calvin taught the principle of *Scriptura tota* and *Scriptura sola*, the whole Scripture and nothing but Scripture. Man must teach all that God revealed, including predestination. But he must not go beyond Scripture, speculating where God has not revealed. We can have no finer attitude to follow than this expressed by Calvin.

---

[4]Calvin, III, xxi, 4. The translation used here is largely the one done by Ford Battles, published by the Westminster Press in 1960.

The Belgic Confession of Faith (1561)

ARTICLE XIII

THE PROVIDENCE OF GOD AND HIS GOVERNMENT
OF ALL THINGS

We believe that the same good God, after He had created all things, did not forsake them or give them up to fortune or chance, but that He rules and governs them according to His holy will, so that nothing happens in this world without His appointment; nevertheless, God neither is the Author of nor can be charged with the sins which are committed. For His power and goodness are so great and incomprehensible that He orders and executes His work in the most excellent and just manner, even then when devils and wicked men act unjustly. And as to what He does surpassing human understanding, we will not curiously inquire into farther than our capacity will admit of; but with the greatest humility and reverence adore the righteous judgments of God, which are hid from us, contenting ourselves that we are pupils of Christ, to learn only those things which He has revealed to us in His Word, without transgressing these limits.

This doctrine affords us unspeakable consolation, since we are taught thereby that nothing can befall us by chance, but by the direction of our most gracious and heavenly Father; who watches over us with a paternal care, keeping all creatures so under His power that *not a hair of our head (for they are all numbered), nor a sparrow can fall to the ground without the will of our Father,* in whom we do entirely trust; being persuaded that He so restrains the devil and all our enemies that without His will and permission they cannot hurt us.

And therefore we reject that damnable error of the Epicureans, who say that God regards nothing but leaves all things to chance.

ARTICLE XIV

THE CREATION AND FALL OF MAN, AND HIS INCAPACITY TO
PERFORM WHAT IS TRULY GOOD

We believe that God created man out of the dust of the earth, and made and formed him after His own image and likeness, good, righteous, and holy, capable in all things to will agreeably to the will of God. But *being in honor, he understood it not,* neither knew his excellency, but wilfully subjected himself to sin and consequently to death and the curse, giving ear to the words of the devil. For the commandment of life, which he had received, he transgressed; and by sin separated himself from God, who was his true life; having corrupted his whole nature; whereby he made himself liable to corporal and spiritual death. And being thus become wicked, perverse, and corrupt in all his ways, he has lost all his excellent gifts which he had received from God, and retained only small remains thereof, which, however, are sufficient to leave man without excuse; for all the light which is in us is changed into darkness, as the Scriptures teach us, saying: *The light shineth in the darkness, and the darkness apprehended it not;* where St. John calls men darkness.

Therefore we reject all that is taught repugnant to this concerning the free will of man, since man is but a slave to sin, and *can receive nothing, except it have been given him from heaven.* For who may presume to boast that he of himself can do any good, since Christ says: *No man can come to me, except the Father that sent me draw him?* Who will glory in his own will, who understands that *the mind of the flesh is enmity against God?* Who can speak of his knowledge, since *the natural man receiveth not the things of the Spirit of God?* In short, who dare suggest any thought, since he knows that we *are not sufficient of ourselves to account anything as of ourselves, but that our sufficiency is of God?* And therefore what the apostle says ought justly to be held sure and firm, that *God worketh in us both to will and to work, for his good pleasure.* For there is no understanding nor will conformable to the divine understanding and will but what Christ has wrought in man; which He teaches us, when He says: *Apart from me ye can do nothing.*

ARTICLE XV

ORIGINAL SIN

We believe that through the disobedience of Adam original sin is extended to all mankind; which is a corruption of the whole nature and a hereditary disease, wherewith even infants in their mother's womb are infected, and which produces in man all sorts of sin, being in him as a root thereof, and therefore is so vile and abominable in the sight of God that it is sufficient to condemn all mankind. Nor is it altogether abolished or wholly eradicated even by baptism; since sin always issues forth from this woeful source, as water from a fountain; notwithstanding it is not imputed to the children of God unto condemnation, but by His grace and mercy is forgiven them. Not that they should rest securely in sin, but that a sense of this corruption should make believers often to sigh, desiring to be delivered from this body of death.

Wherefore we reject the error of the Pelagians, who assert that sin proceeds only from imitation.

ARTICLE XVI

ETERNAL ELECTION

We believe that, all the posterity of Adam being thus fallen into perdition and ruin by the sin of our first parents, God then did manifest Himself such as He is; that is to say, merciful and just: **merciful,** since He delivers and preserves from this perdition all whom He in His eternal and unchangeable counsel of mere goodness has elected in Christ Jesus our Lord, without any respect to their works; **just,** in leaving others in the fall and perdition wherein they have involved themselves.

The Westminster Confession of Faith (1648)

CHAPTER III

OF GOD'S ETERNAL DECREE

I God, from all eternity, did, by the most wise and holy counsel of His own will, freely, and unchangeably ordain whatsoever comes to pass: yet so, as thereby neither is God the author of sin, nor is violence offered to the will of the creatures; nor is the liberty or contingency of second causes taken away, but rather established.

II Although God knows whatsoever may or can come to pass on all supposed conditions, yet He has not decreed anything because He foresaw it as future, or as that which would come to pass on such conditions.

III By the decree of God, for the manifestation of His glory, some men and angels are predestinated to everlasting life; and others foreordained to everlasting death.

IV These angels and men, thus predestinated and foreordained, are particularly and unchangeably designed, and their number so certain and definite that it cannot be either increased or diminished.

V Those of mankind that are predestinated to life, God, before the foundation of the world was laid, according to His eternal and immutable purpose, and the secret counsel and good pleasure of His will, has chosen, in Christ, to everlasting glory, out of His mere free grace and love, without any foresight of faith, or good works, or perseverance in either of them, or any other thing in the creature, as conditions, or causes moving Him thereunto; and all to the praise of His glorious grace.

VI As God has appointed the elect to glory, so has He, by the eternal and most free purpose of His will, foreordained all the means thereunto. Wherefore, they who are elected, being fallen in Adam, are redeemed by Christ, are effectually called to faith in Christ by His Spirit working in due season, are justified, adopted, sanctified, and kept by His power, through faith, to salvation. Neither are any other redeemed by Christ, effectually called, justified, adopted, sanctified, and saved, but the elect only.

VII The rest of mankind God was pleased, according to the unsearchable counsel of His own will, whereby He extends or withholds mercy, as He pleases, for the glory of His sovereign power over His creatures, to pass by; and to ordain them to dishonor and wrath for their sin, to the praise of His glorious justice.

VIII The doctrine of this high mystery of predestination is to be handled with special prudence and care, that men, attending the will of God revealed in His Word, and yielding obedience thereunto, may, from the certainty of their effectual vocation, be assured of their eternal election. So shall this doctrine afford matter of praise, reverence, and admiration of God; and of humility, diligence, and abundant consolation to all that sincerely obey the Gospel.

CHAPTER V

OF PROVIDENCE

I God the great Creator of all things does uphold, direct, dispose, and govern all creatures, actions, and things, from the greatest even to the least, by His most wise and holy providence, according to His infallible foreknowledge, and the free and immutable counsel of His own will, to the praise of the glory of His wisdom, power, justice, goodness, and mercy.

II Although, in relation to the foreknowledge and decree of God, the first Cause, all things come to pass immutably and infallibly; yet, by the same providence He orders them to fall out according to the nature of second causes, either necessarily, freely, or contingently.

III God, in His ordinary providence, makes use of means, yet is free to work without, above, and against them, at His pleasure.

IV The almighty power, unsearchable wisdom, and infinite goodness of God so far manifest themselves in His providence, that it extends itself to the first fall, and all other sins of angels and men; and that not by a bare permission, but such as has joined with it a most wise and powerful bounding, and otherwise ordering, and governing of them in a manifold dispensation, to His own holy ends; yet so, as the sinfulness thereof proceeds only from the creature, and not from God, who, being most holy and righteous, neither is nor can be the author or approver of sin.

V The most wise, righteous, and gracious God does oftentimes leave for a season His own children to manifold temptations and the corruption of their own hearts, to chastise them for their former sins, or to discover to them the hidden strength of corruption and deceitfulness of their hearts, that they may be humbled; and to raise them to a more close and constant dependence for their support upon Himself, and to make them more watchful against all future occasions of sin, and for sundry other just and holy ends.

VI As for those wicked and ungodly men whom God, as a righteous Judge, for former sins, does blind and harden, from them He not only withholds His grace whereby they might have been enlightened in their understandings, and wrought upon in their hearts; but sometimes also withdraws the gifts which they had, and exposes them to such objects as their corruption makes occasions of sin; and, withal, gives them over to their own lusts, the temptations of the world, and the power of Satan, whereby it comes to pass that they harden themselves, even under those means which God uses for the softening of others.

VII As the providence of God does in general reach to all creatures; so, after a most special manner, it takes care of His Church, and disposes all things to the good thereof.

CHAPTER VI

OF THE FALL OF MAN, OF SIN, AND OF THE PUNISHMENT THEREOF

I Our first parents, being seduced by the subtilty and temptation of Satan, sinned in eating the forbidden fruit. This their sin God was pleased, according to His wise and holy counsel, to permit, having purposed to order it to His own glory.

II By this sin they fell from their original righteousness and communion with God, and so became dead in sin and wholly defiled in all the parts and faculties of soul and body.

III They being the root of all mankind, the guilt of this sin was imputed; and the same death in sin, and corrupted nature, conveyed to all their posterity descending from them by ordinary generation.

IV From this original corruption, whereby we are utterly indisposed, disabled, and made opposite to all good, and wholly inclined to all evil, do proceed all actual transgressions.

V This corruption of nature, during this life, does remain in those that are regenerated; and although it be, through Christ, pardoned and mortified; yet both itself, and all the motions thereof, are truly and properly sin.

VI Every sin, both original and actual, being a transgression of the righteous law of God, and contrary thereunto, does in its own nature bring guilt upon the sinner, whereby he is bound over to the wrath of God, and curse of the law, and so made subject to death with all miseries spiritual, temporal, and eternal.

CHAPTER VII

OF GOD'S COVENANT WITH MAN

II The first covenant made with man was a covenant of works, wherein life was promised to Adam; and in him to his posterity, upon condition of perfect and personal obedience.

III Man, by his fall, having made himself uncapable of life by that covenant, the Lord was pleased to make a second, commonly called the covenant of grace; wherein He freely offers to sinners life and salvation by Jesus Christ; requiring of them faith in Him, that they may be saved, and promising to give to all those that are ordained to eternal life His Holy Spirit, to make them willing, and able to believe.

CHAPTER VIII

OF CHRIST THE MEDIATOR

I It pleased God, in His eternal purpose, to choose and ordain the Lord Jesus, His only begotten Son, to be the Mediator between God and man, the Prophet, Priest, and King, the Head and Savior of His Church, the Heir of all things, and Judge of the world: to whom He did from all eternity give a people, to be His seed, and to be by Him in time redeemed, called, justified, sanctified, and glorified.

V The Lord Jesus, by His perfect obedience, and sacrifice of Himself, which He, through the eternal Spirit, once offered up to God, has fully satisfied the justice of His Father; and purchased, not only reconciliation, but an everlasting inheritance in the kingdom of heaven, for all those whom the Father has given to Him.

VIII To all those for whom Christ has purchased redemption, He does certainly and effectually apply and communicate the same; making intercession for them and revealing to them, in and by the Word, the mysteries of salvation; effectually persuading them by His Spirit to believe and obey, and governing their hearts by His Word and Spirit; overcoming all their enemies by His almighty power and wisdom, in such manner and ways, as are most consonant to His wonderful and unsearchable dispensation.

CHAPTER IX

OF FREE-WILL

I God has endued the will of man with that natural liberty, that it is neither forced, nor, by any absolute necessity of nature, determined to good, or evil.

II Man, in his state of innocency, had freedom and power to will and to do that which was good and well pleasing to God; but yet, mutably, so that he might fall from it.

III Man, by his fall into a state of sin, has wholly lost all ability of will to any spiritual good accompanying salvation: so as, a natural man, being altogether averse from that good, and dead in sin, is not able by his own strength to convert himself, or to prepare himself thereunto.

IV When God converts a sinner and translates him into the state of grace, He frees him from his natural bondage under sin; and, by His grace alone, enables him freely to will and to do that which is spiritually good; yet so, as that by reason of his remaining corruption, he does not perfectly, nor only, will that which is good, but does also will that which is evil.

V The will of man is made perfectly and immutably free to good alone in the state of glory only.

CHAPTER X

OF EFFECTUAL CALLING

I All those whom God has predestinated to life, and those only, He is pleased, in His appointed and accepted time, effectually to call, by His Word and Spirit, out of that state of sin and death, in which they are by nature, to grace and salvation, by Jesus Christ; enlightening their minds spiritually and savingly to understand the things of God, taking away their heart of stone, and giving to them a heart of flesh; renewing their wills, and by His almighty power determining them to that which is good, and effectually drawing them to Jesus Christ; yet so, as they come most freely, being made willing by His grace.

II This effectual call is of God's free and special grace alone, not from anything at all foreseen in man, who is altogether passive therein, until, being made alive and renewed by the Holy Spirit, he is thereby enabled to answer this call, and to embrace the grace offered and conveyed in it.

III Elect infants, dying in infancy, are regenerated, and saved by Christ, through the Spirit, who works when and where and how He pleases; so also are all other elect persons who are uncapable of being outwardly called by the ministry of the Word.

IV Others, not elected, although they may be called by the ministry of the Word, and may have some common operations of the Spirit, yet they never truly come to Christ, and therefore cannot be saved; much less can men, not professing the Christian religion, be saved in any other way whatsoever, be they never so diligent to frame their lives according to the light of nature, and the laws of that religion they do profess. And, to assert and maintain that they may, is very pernicious, and to be detested.

CHAPTER XIV

OF SAVING FAITH

I The grace of faith, whereby the elect are enabled to believe to the saving of their souls, is the work of the Spirit of Christ in their hearts, and is ordinarily wrought by the ministry of the Word, by which also, and by the administration of the sacraments, and prayer, it is increased and strengthened.

CHAPTER XVI

OF GOOD WORKS

I Good works are only such as God has commanded in His holy Word, and not such as, without the warrant thereof, are devised by men, out of blind zeal, or on any pretence of good intention.

II These good works, done in obedience to God's commandments, are the fruits and evidences of a true and lively faith; and by them believers manifest their thankfulness, strengthen their assurance, edify their brethren, adorn the profession of the Gospel, stop the mouths of the adversaries, and glorify God, whose workmanship they are, created in Christ Jesus thereunto, that, having their fruit unto holiness, they may have the end, eternal life.

III Their ability to do good works is not at all of themselves, but wholly from the Spirit of Christ. And that they may be enabled thereunto, beside the graces they have already received, there is required an actual influence of the same Holy Spirit, to work in them to will, and to do, of His good pleasure; yet are they not hereupon to grow negligent, as if they were not bound to perform any duty unless upon a special motion of the Spirit; but they ought to be diligent in stirring up the grace of God that is in them.

VII Works done by unregenerate men, although for the matter of them they may be things which God commands; and of good use both to themselves and others; yet, because they proceed not from a heart purified by faith, nor are done in a right manner, according to the Word, nor to a right end, the glory of God, they are therefore sinful, and cannot please God, or make a man meet to receive grace from God; and yet, the neglect of them is more sinful and displeasing to God.

CHAPTER XVII

OF THE PERSEVERANCE OF THE SAINTS

I They, whom God has accepted in His Beloved, effectually called, and sanctified by His Spirit, can neither totally nor finally fall away from the state of grace, but shall certainly persevere therein to the end, and be eternally saved.

II This perseverance of the saints depends not on their own free will, but on the immutability of the decree of election, flowing from the free and unchangeable love of God the Father; on the efficacy of the merit and intercession of Jesus Christ, the abiding of the Spirit, and of the seed of God within them, and the nature of the covenant of grace; from all which arises also the certainty and infallibility thereof.

III Nevertheless, they may, through the temptations of Satan and of the world, the prevalency of corruption remaining in them, and the neglect of the means of their preservation, fall into grievous sins, and, for a time, continue therein; whereby they incur God's displeasure, and grieve His Holy Spirit, come to be deprived of some measure of their graces and comforts, have their hearts hardened, and their consciences wounded, hurt and scandalize others, and bring temporal judgments on themselves.

The Heidelberg Catechism (1563)

QUESTION AND ANSWER 26

Question: What do you believe when you say: *I believe in God the Father, Almighty, maker of heaven and earth?*

Answer: That the eternal Father of our Lord Jesus Christ, who out of nothing created heaven and earth and everything in them, who still upholds and rules them by His eternal counsel and providence, is my God and Father because of Christ His Son. I trust Him so much I do not doubt He will provide whatever I need for body and soul, and He will turn to my good whatever adversity He sends me in this sad world. He is able to do this because He is almighty God; He desires to do this because He is a faithful Father.

QUESTION AND ANSWER 27

Question: What do you understand by the providence of God?

Answer: Providence is the almighty and ever-present power of God by which He upholds, as with His hand, heaven and earth and all creatures, and so rules them that leaf and blade, rain and drought, fruitful and lean years, food and drink, health and sickness, prosperity and poverty—all things, in fact—come to us not by chance but from His fatherly hand.

QUESTION AND ANSWER 28

Question: How does the knowledge of God's creation and providence help us?

Answer: We can be patient when things go against us, thankful when things go well, and for the future we can have good confidence in our faithful God and Father that nothing will separate us from His love. All creatures are so completely in His hand that without His will they can neither move nor be moved.

bibliography

Bavinck, H. *The Doctrine of God.* Grand Rapids: Wm. B. Eerdmans Publishing Co., 1951. For the theologically mature.

Berkouwer, G. C. *Divine Election.* Grand Rapids: Wm. B. Eerdmans Publishing Co., 1960. 336 pp. For the theologically advanced.

Boettner, Loraine. *The Reformed Doctrine of Predestination.* Philadelphia: Presbyterian and Reformed Publishing Co., 1963. 435 pp. The best for beginners. Very lucid, full, and well organized.

Calvin, John. *Calvin's Calvinism.* Grand Rapids: Wm. B. Eerdmans Publishing Co., 1950. 350 pp. Slow reading, but it deals clearly with foreordination of sin.

Calvin, John. *Institutes of the Christian Religion,* III, xxi-xxiv. A gold mine. Moderately difficult, but unsurpassable.

Klooster, Fred. *Calvin's Doctrine of Predestination.* Grand Rapids: Calvin Theological Seminary, 1961. 77 pp. A most worthwhile paperback with many full quotes from Calvin. Not easy, but not too hard, either.

Luther, Martin. *The Bondage of the Will.* Translated by J. I. Packer and O. R. Johnston. Westwood, N. J.: Fleming Revell Co., 1957. Luther at his best. Blunt, lively, clear.

Packer, J. I. *Evangelism and the Sovereignty of God.* Chicago: Inter-Varsity Press, 1961. 126 pp. An excellent, practical paperback. One of the best.

Pink, A. W. *The Sovereignty of God.* Grand Rapids: Baker Book House, Reprint 1965. Plain, full, practical.

Spurgeon, C. H. *Sermons on Sovereignty.* Warm, plain.

Stickelberger, Emanuel. *Calvin: A Life.* Richmond, Va.: John Knox Press, 1954. This is an outstanding, brief (174 pp.) biography.